Big Book of Indian Beadwork Designs

Kay Doherty Bennett

DOVER PUBLICATIONS, INC.
Mineola, New York

Bibliographical Note

This Dover edition, first published in 1999, is a new selection of patterns from *Designs for Beadwork, Applique & Embroidery, Vols. 1–4*, first published by Pencil Bend Design Co., Kettle Falls, Washington and Seattle, Washington, 1987–1994. A new Note has been written for this edition.

Library of Congress Cataloging-in-Publication Data

Bennett, Kay Doherty.
    Big book of Indian beadwork designs / Kay Doherty Bennett.
         p.   cm.
    Reprint. Originally published under title: Designs for beadwork, applique & embroidery. Kettle Falls, Wash. and Seattle, Wash. : Pencil Bend Design Co., 1987–1994.
    ISBN-13: 978-0-486-40283-3 (pbk.)
    ISBN-10: 0-486-40283-5 (pbk.)
    1. Beadwork—Patterns.   2. Indian beadwork—North America.   3. Appliqué—Patterns.
I. Title
TT860.B463   1999
745.58'2—dc21

                                                98-52998
                                                       CIP

Manufactured in the United States by LSC Communications
40283510   2019
www.doverpublications.com

Note

This book contains over 300 beadwork designs, both for weaving and appliqué. The vast majority were inspired by the work of Native American peoples from all over the continent, from the northeast and west through Mexico. The designs can be used for belts (in any width), hatbands, bracelets, pouches, clothing, and many other articles. There are florals, animals, geometrics, kachinas, Mayan designs, and more.

Instructions for bead weaving and appliqué are widely available, so we have chosen to fill the pages with designs rather than instructions. Bead weaving designs are shown on an elliptical, rather than a square grid, giving a truer picture of the finished piece. Color codes are included for all charts. Appliqué designs can be enlarged or reduced as needed using a photocopier.

ALL DESIGNS ARE 7 BEADS WIDE ON THIS PAGE. WORK LEFT TO RIGHT, RETURN TO ARROWS AND REPEAT.

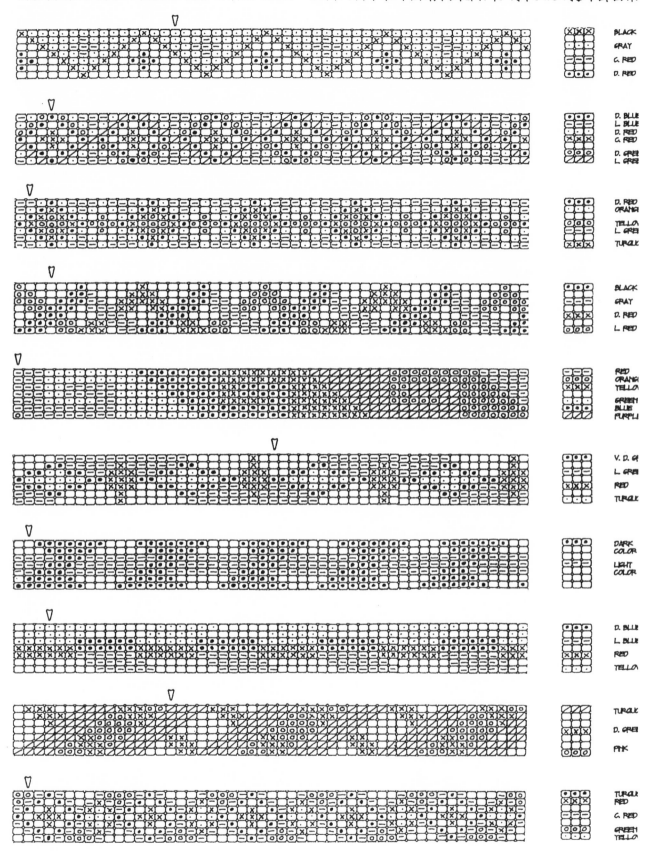

THESE NARROW BANDS ARE GOOD FOR HATBANDS, BELTS, BRACELETS, ANKLETS OR POCKET

WORK LEFT TO RIGHT. RETURN TO ARROWS. REPEAT UNTIL IT IS THE DESIRED LENGTH.

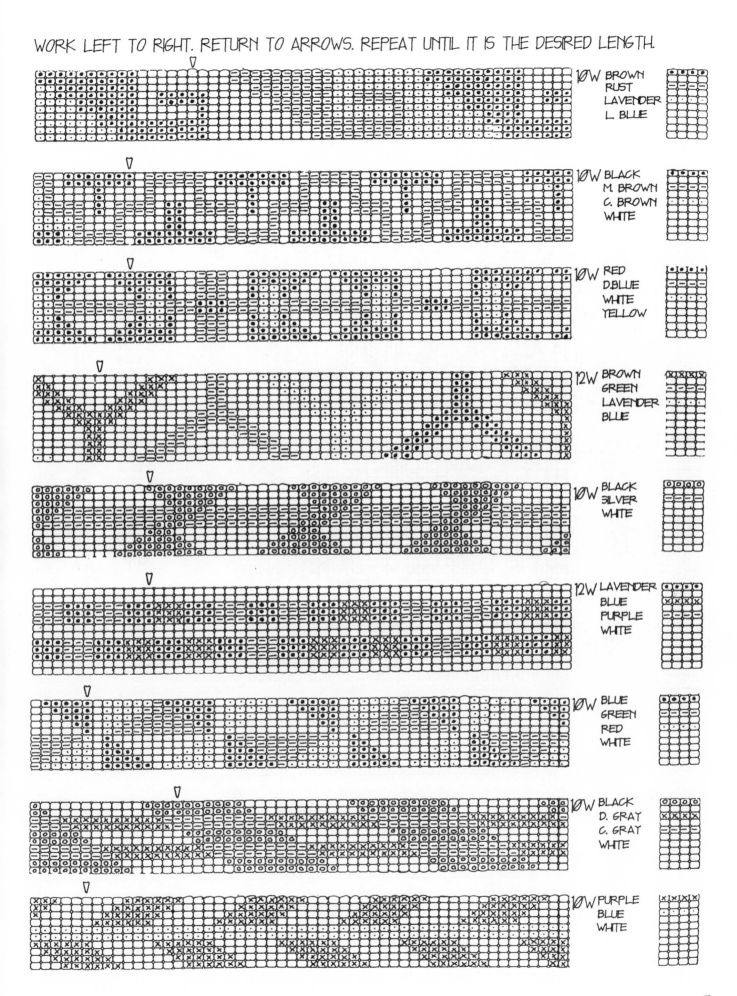

10W BROWN
RUST
LAVENDER
L. BLUE

10W BLACK
M. BROWN
C. BROWN
WHITE

10W RED
D. BLUE
WHITE
YELLOW

12W BROWN
GREEN
LAVENDER
BLUE

10W BLACK
SILVER
WHITE

12W LAVENDER
BLUE
PURPLE
WHITE

10W BLUE
GREEN
RED
WHITE

10W BLACK
D. GRAY
C. GRAY
WHITE

10W PURPLE
BLUE
WHITE

WORK LEFT TO RIGHT. RETURN TO ARROWS. REPEAT UNTIL IT IS THE DESIRED LENGTH.

9W — BLUE / RED / GREEN / WHITE

9W — D. PURPLE / L. PURPLE / D. BLUE / WHITE

10W — D. BLUE / YELLOW / GREEN / WHITE

10W — D. BLUE / L. BLUE / RED / GREEN / PINK

10W — BROWN / M. BLUE / L. BLUE / GREEN

10W — BLACK / BROWN / C. BROWN / WHITE

10W — M. RED / L. RED / GRAY / BLACK / WHITE

10W — D. BLUE / L. BLUE / RED / YELLOW

11W — D.BLUE / L. BLUE / YELLOW / WHITE

12W — D. PURPLE / L. PURPLE / D. BLUE / L. GREEN

ALL DESIGNS ARE 11 BEADS WIDE ON THIS PAGE. WORK LEFT TO RIGHT, RETURN TO ARROWS AND REPEAT.

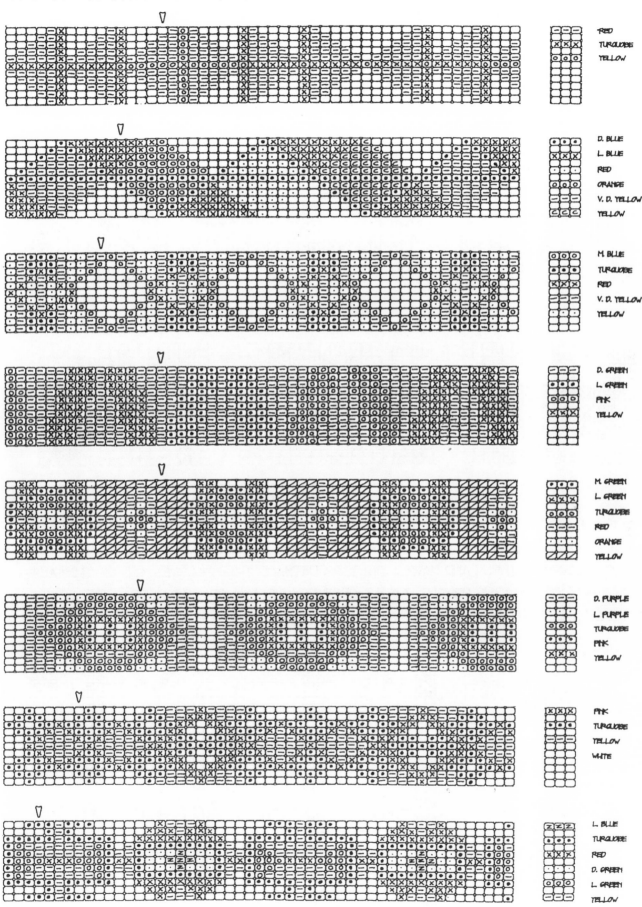

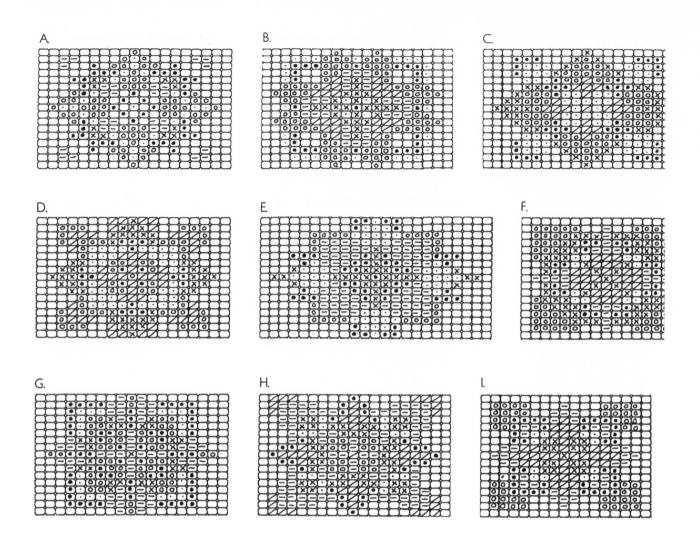

A.   B.   C.

D.   E.   F.

G.   H.   I.

ALL OF THE DESIGNS ON THIS PAGE ARE 17 BEADS WIDE. WORK FROM LEFT TO RIGHT.
ON THE NEXT PAGE DESIGNS A THRU D ARE GRAPHED REPETITIVELY WITH THEIR COLOR CODES.
OR LOOM DESIGNS A THRU I AND HAVE A BELT OR HATBAND THAT INCLUDES ALL OF THE DESIG
USE A ZEROX TO COPY THE DESIGNS. USE COLORED PENCILS TO WORK OUT YOUR CHOICE OF COL
ANY BEADS THAT ARE UNMARKED ARE WHITE.

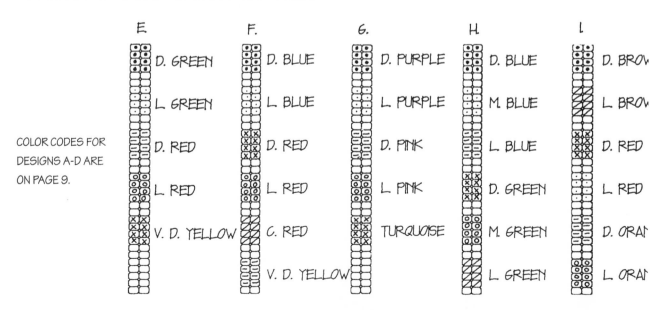

COLOR CODES FOR
DESIGNS A-D ARE
ON PAGE 9.

E.	F.	G.	H.	I.
D. GREEN	D. BLUE	D. PURPLE	D. BLUE	D. BROW
L. GREEN	L. BLUE	L. PURPLE	M. BLUE	L. BROW
D. RED	D. RED	D. PINK	L. BLUE	D. RED
L. RED	L. RED	L. PINK	D. GREEN	L. RED
V. D. YELLOW	C. RED	TURQUOISE	M. GREEN	D. ORAÏ
	V. D. YELLOW		L. GREEN	L. ORAÏ

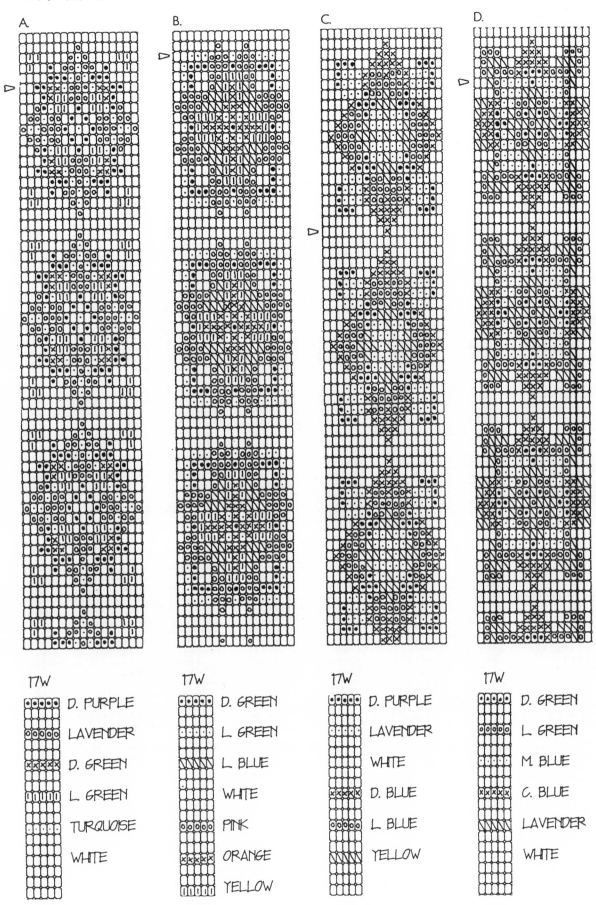

A.

17W

••••	D. PURPLE
○○○○	LAVENDER
××××	D. GREEN
llll	L. GREEN
	TURQUOISE
	WHITE

B.

17W

•••••	D. GREEN
	L. GREEN
\\\\	L. BLUE
	WHITE
○○○○	PINK
××××	ORANGE
llllll	YELLOW

C.

17W

•○○○•	D. PURPLE
	LAVENDER
	WHITE
××××	D. BLUE
○○○○	L. BLUE
\\\\	YELLOW

D.

17W

○○○○○	D. GREEN
○○○○	L. GREEN
	M. BLUE
××××	C. BLUE
\\\\	LAVENDER
	WHITE

9

START AT THE TOP. WORK TO BOTTOM. RETURN TO ARROWS. REPEAT UNTIL IT IS THE DESIRED LEN

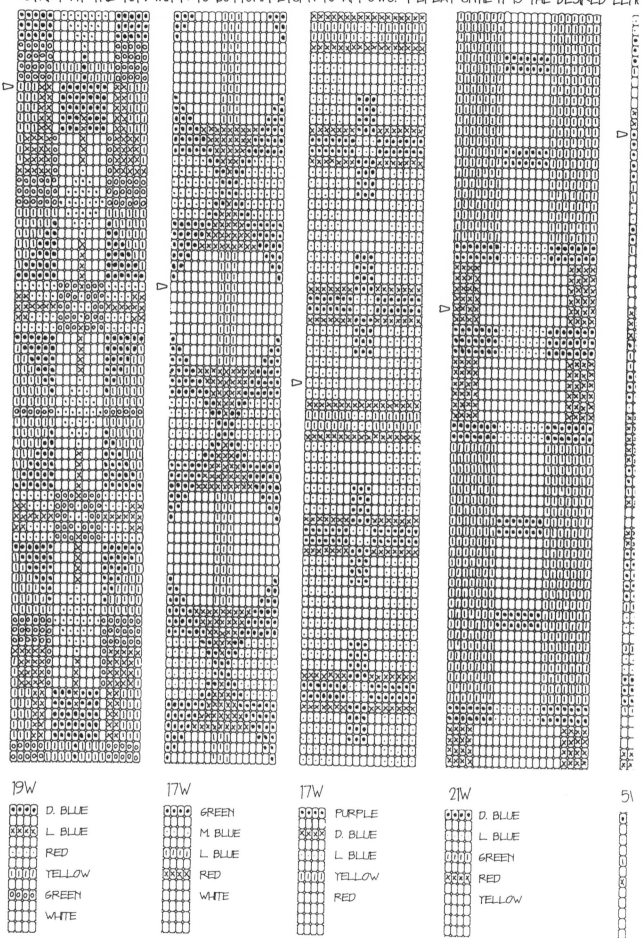

19W

●●●●	D. BLUE
××××	L BLUE
	RED
00000	YELLOW
○○○○	GREEN
	WHITE

17W

●●●●	GREEN
	M. BLUE
0000	L BLUE
××××	RED
	WHITE

17W

●●●●	PURPLE
××××	D. BLUE
	L BLUE
0000	YELLOW
	RED

21W

●●●●	D. BLUE
	L BLUE
0000	GREEN
××××	RED
	YELLOW

5\

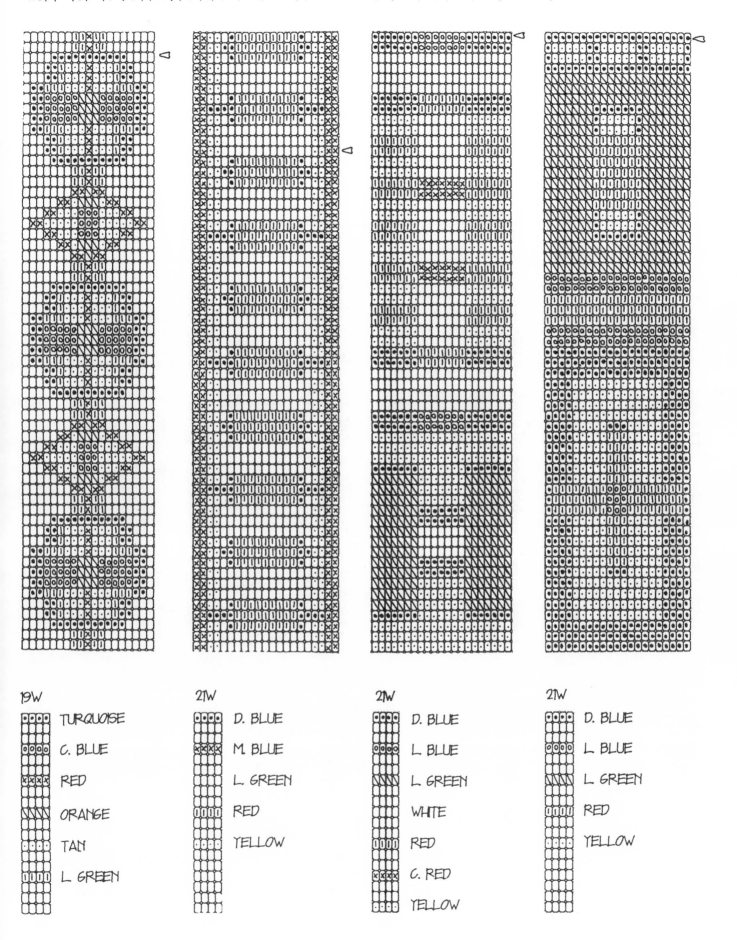

19W

▣▣▣▣	TURQUOISE
◎◎◎◎	C. BLUE
✕✕✕✕	RED
⧄⧄⧄⧄	ORANGE
••••	TAN
▯▯▯▯	L. GREEN

21W

◎◎◎◎	D. BLUE
✕✕✕✕	M. BLUE
⧄⧄⧄⧄	L. GREEN
▯▯▯▯	RED
••••	YELLOW

21W

▣▣▣▣	D. BLUE
◎◎◎◎	L. BLUE
⧄⧄⧄⧄	L. GREEN
▯▯▯▯	WHITE
▯▯▯▯	RED
✕✕✕✕	C. RED
▤▤▤▤	YELLOW

21W

▣▣▣▣	D. BLUE
◎◎◎◎	L. BLUE
⧄⧄⧄⧄	L. GREEN
▯▯▯▯	RED
••••	YELLOW

11

WORK TOP TO BOTTOM, RETURN TO THE ARROWS AND REPEAT UNTIL IT IS THE DESIRED LENGTH.

WORK THIS STRIP TOP TO
GO TO ARROW AND WO
TO THE TOP. THIS WILL
THREE FULL TRIANGLES.

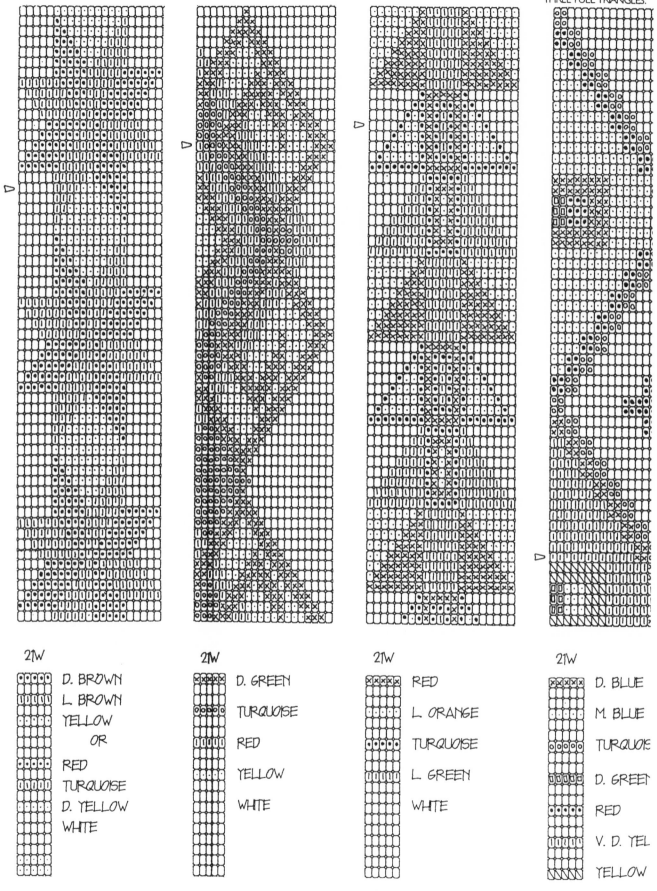

21W

	D. BROWN
	L. BROWN
	YELLOW
	OR
	RED
	TURQUOISE
	D. YELLOW
	WHITE

21W

	D. GREEN
	TURQUOISE
	RED
	YELLOW
	WHITE

21W

	RED
	L. ORANGE
	TURQUOISE
	L. GREEN
	WHITE

21W

	D. BLUE
	M. BLUE
	TURQUOISE
	D. GREEN
	RED
	V. D. YEL
	YELLOW

27W

[•••] RED		[ooo] BLUE
[|||] D. GREEN		[xxx] C. BLUE
[ ] L. GREEN		[ ] WHITE

15W

[••] BLUE		[xx] D. GREEN
[·] TURQUOISE		[||] L. GREEN
[cc] RED		[ ] YELLOW

25W

[•••] PURPLE		[|||] L. BROWN
[|||] BLUE		
[ ] WHITE		

22W

[•••] BLACK		[|||] LAVENDER
[xxx] RED		[ooo] D. BROWN
[ ] L. BLUE		[ ] WHITE

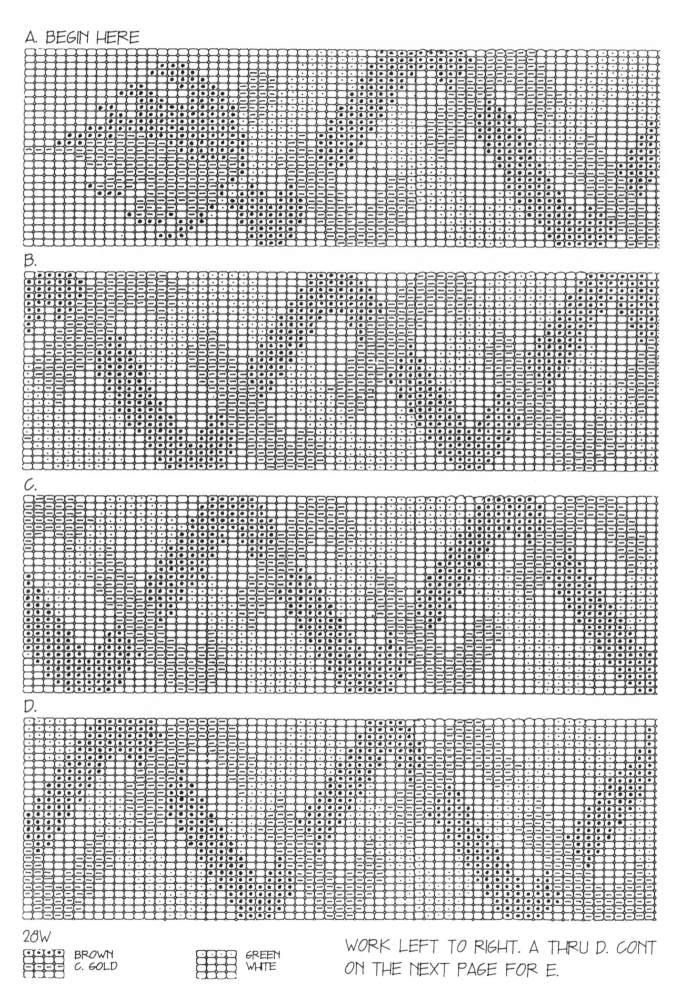

A. BEGIN HERE

B.

C.

D.

28W

| | BROWN C. GOLD |
| | GREEN WHITE |

WORK LEFT TO RIGHT. A THRU D. CONT
ON THE NEXT PAGE FOR E.

E.

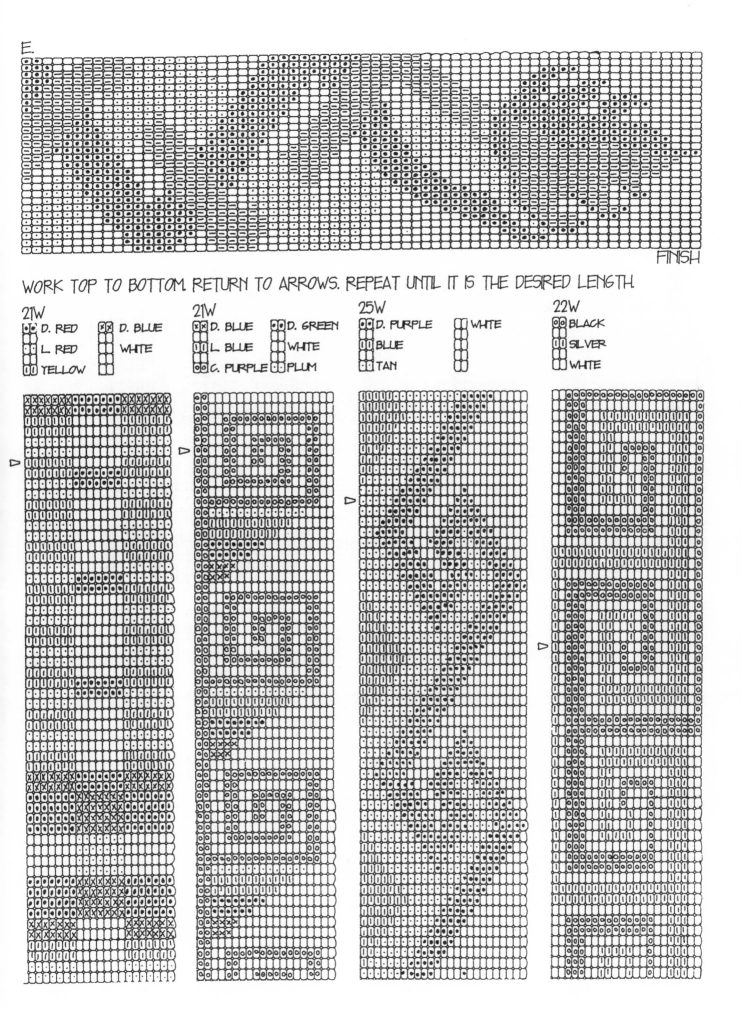

FINISH

WORK TOP TO BOTTOM. RETURN TO ARROWS. REPEAT UNTIL IT IS THE DESIRED LENGTH.

21W
D. RED   D. BLUE
L. RED   WHITE
YELLOW

21W
D. BLUE   D. GREEN
L. BLUE   WHITE
C. PURPLE   PLUM

25W
D. PURPLE   WHITE
BLUE
TAN

22W
BLACK
SILVER
WHITE

A. BEGIN HERE

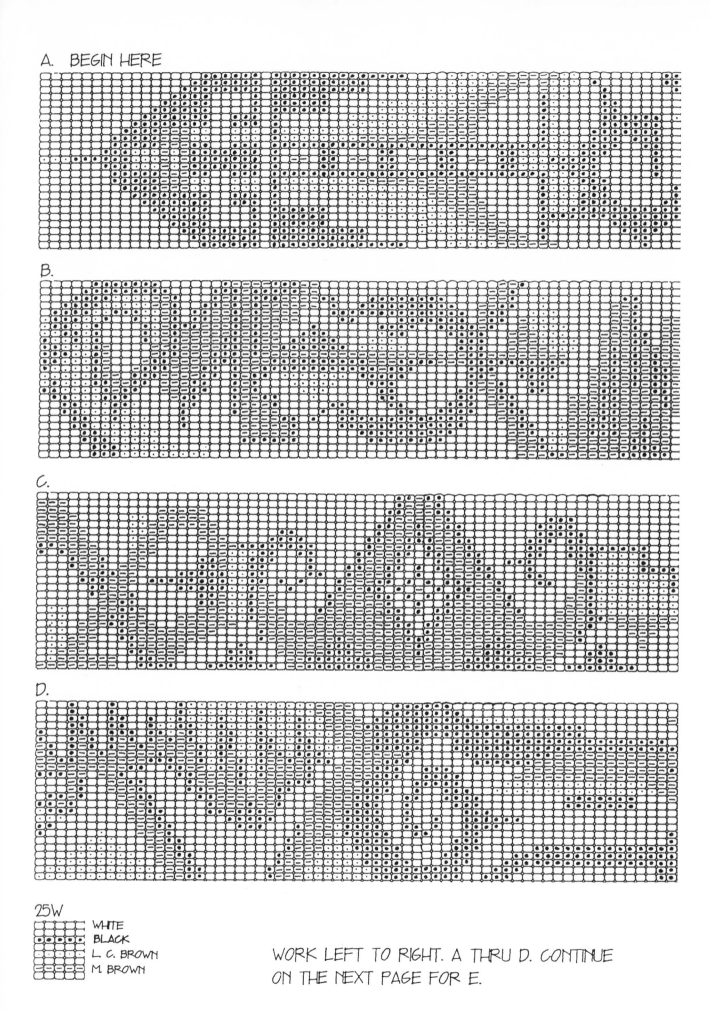

B.

C.

D.

25W

WHITE
BLACK
L. C. BROWN
M. BROWN

WORK LEFT TO RIGHT. A THRU D. CONTINUE
ON THE NEXT PAGE FOR E.

E.

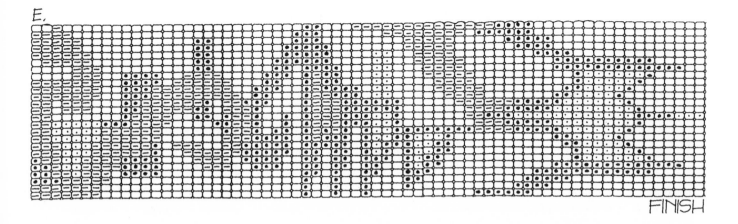

FINISH

WORK BOTTOM TO TOP. RETURN TO ARROWS. REPEAT UNTIL IT IS THE DESIRED LENGTH.

D. BLUE	D. GREEN	BLUE / YELLOW
L. BLUE	L. GREEN	RED / GREEN
L. PURPLE	RUST	/ WHITE
PINK	TURQUOISE	

D. GREEN	CLEAR
TURQUOISE	L. BLUE
D. PURPLE	
M. PURPLE	

BROWN
L. BLUE
GREEN
WHITE

13W   15W   14W   30W   9W

WORK LEFT TO RIGHT. RETURN TO ARROWS. REPEAT UNTIL IT IS THE DESIRED LENGTH.

ALL DESIGNS ON THIS PAGE ARE 25W.

Pattern	Color	Pattern	Color	Pattern	Color
	D. RED		D. GREEN		D. BLUE
	L. RED		M. GREEN		M. BLUE
	YELLOW		BLUE GREEN		TURQUOISE
	PURPLE		WHITE		PINK

WORK LEFT TO RIGHT. RETURN TO ARROWS. REPEAT UNTIL IT IS THE DESIRED LENGTH.

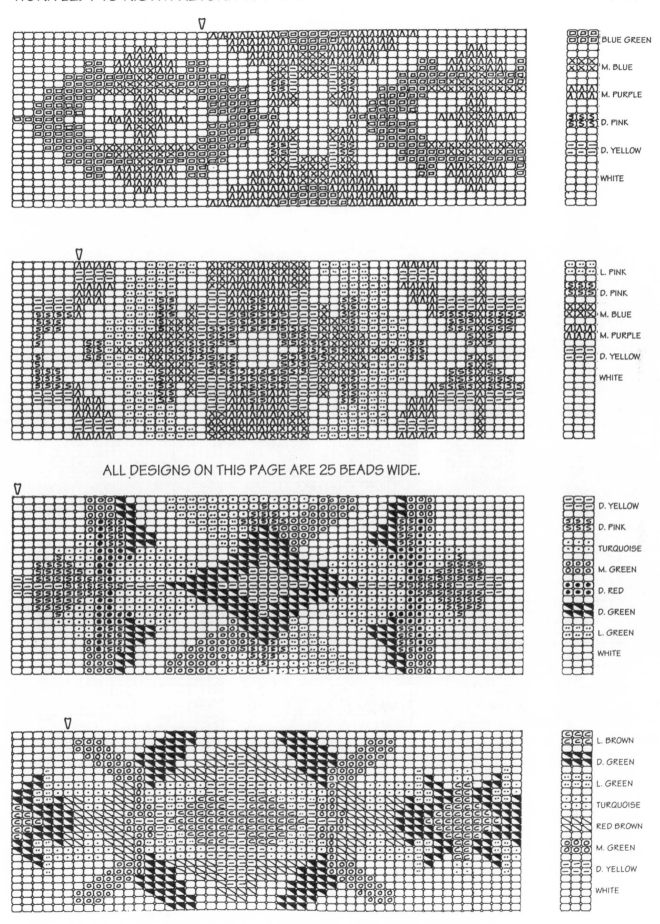

ALL DESIGNS ON THIS PAGE ARE 25 BEADS WIDE.

BLUE GREEN
M. BLUE
M. PURPLE
D. PINK
D. YELLOW
WHITE

L. PINK
D. PINK
M. BLUE
M. PURPLE
D. YELLOW
WHITE

D. YELLOW
D. PINK
TURQUOISE
M. GREEN
D. RED
D. GREEN
L. GREEN
WHITE

L. BROWN
D. GREEN
L. GREEN
TURQUOISE
RED BROWN
M. GREEN
D. YELLOW
WHITE

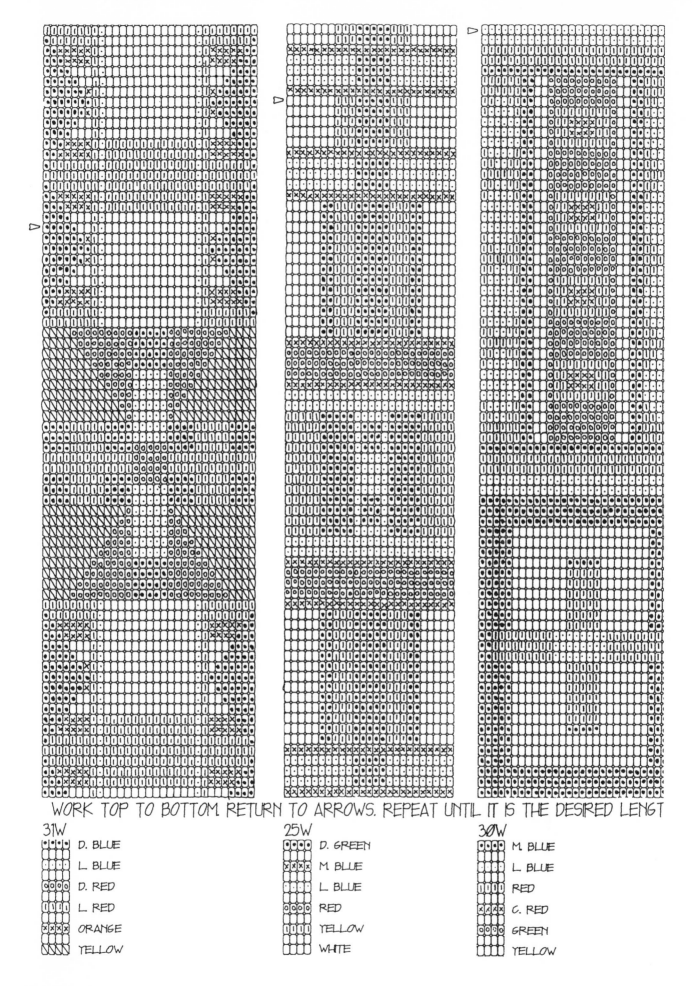

WORK TOP TO BOTTOM. RETURN TO ARROWS. REPEAT UNTIL IT IS THE DESIRED LENGT

31W	
•• ••	D. BLUE
	L BLUE
⊘⊘⊘⊘	D. RED
ⅠⅠⅠⅠ	L RED
✕✕✕	ORANGE
⧄⧄⧄	YELLOW

25W	
•• •	D. GREEN
✕✕✕	M. BLUE
	L BLUE
⊘⊘⊘⊘	RED
ⅠⅠⅠⅠ	YELLOW
	WHITE

30W	
•• •	M. BLUE
	L BLUE
ⅠⅠⅠⅠ	RED
✕✕✕	C. RED
⊘⊘⊘⊘	GREEN
	YELLOW

20

Chart 1

29W

Symbol	Color	Symbol	Color
X X X X	D. GREEN	• • •	D. BLUE
❘❘❘❘	L. GREEN		YELLOW
◦ ◦ ◦	RED		

Chart 2

29W

Symbol	Color	Symbol	Color
❘❘❘❘	GREEN		ORANGE
• • •	D. BLUE		LAVENDER
◦ ◦ ◦	L. BLUE		

Chart 3

29W

Symbol	Color	Symbol	Color
❘❘❘	PINK	＼＼＼	YELLOW
• • •	RED	◦ ◦ ◦	BLACK
❘❘❘❘	WHITE	❘❘❘❘	D. BLUE
X X X X	D. GREEN		L. BLUE

WORK TOP TO BOTTOM. RETURN TO ARROWS. REPEAT UNTIL IT IS THE DESIRED LENGTH.

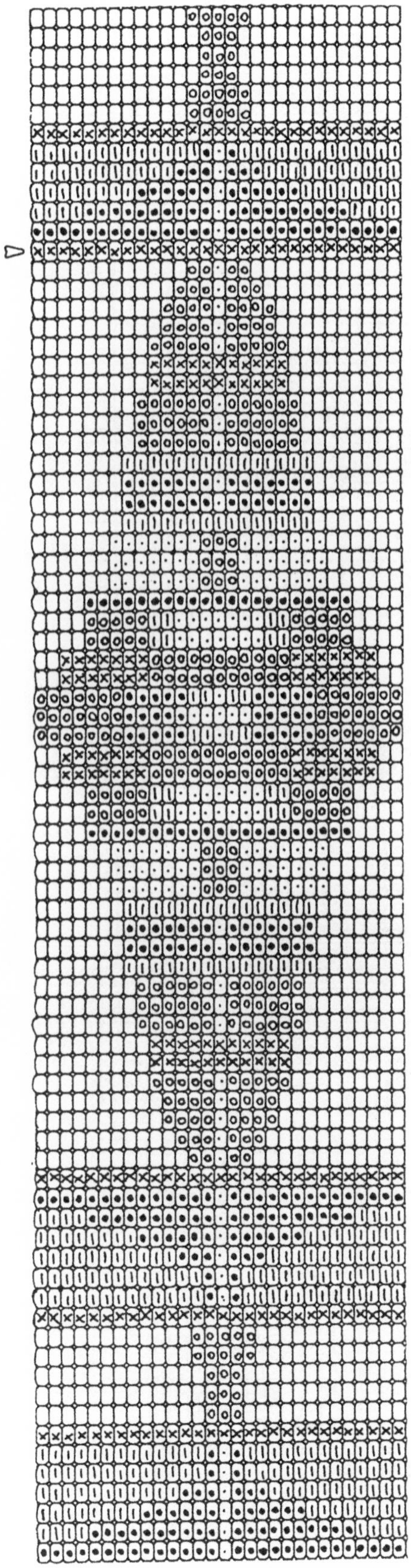

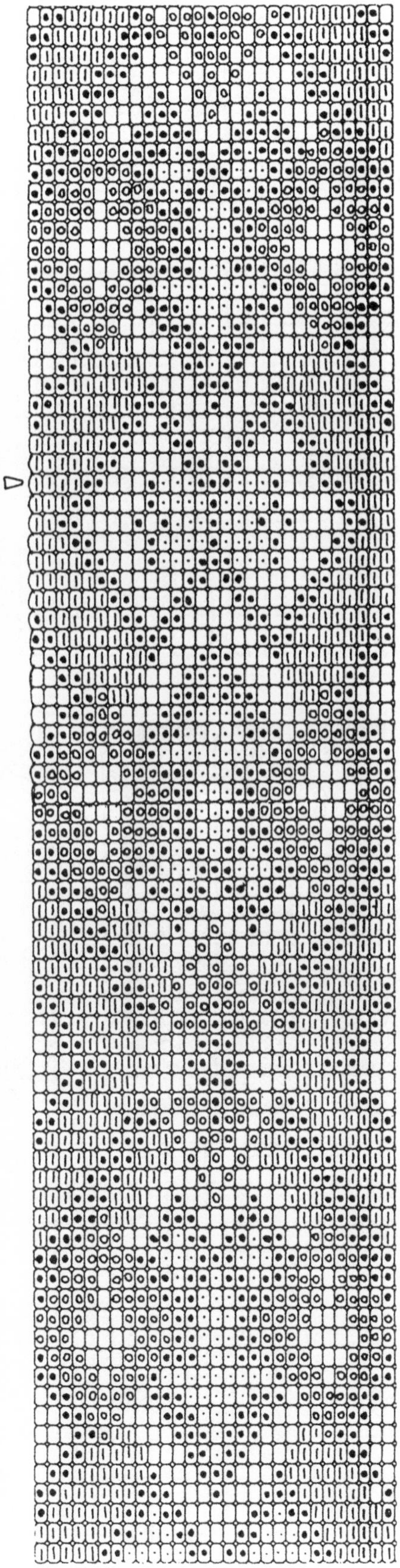

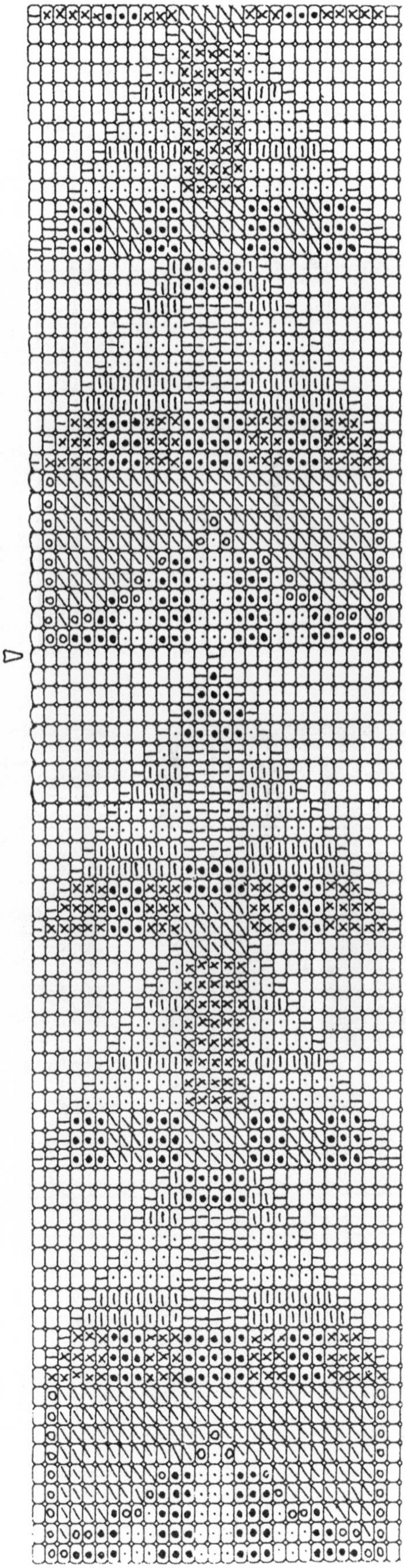

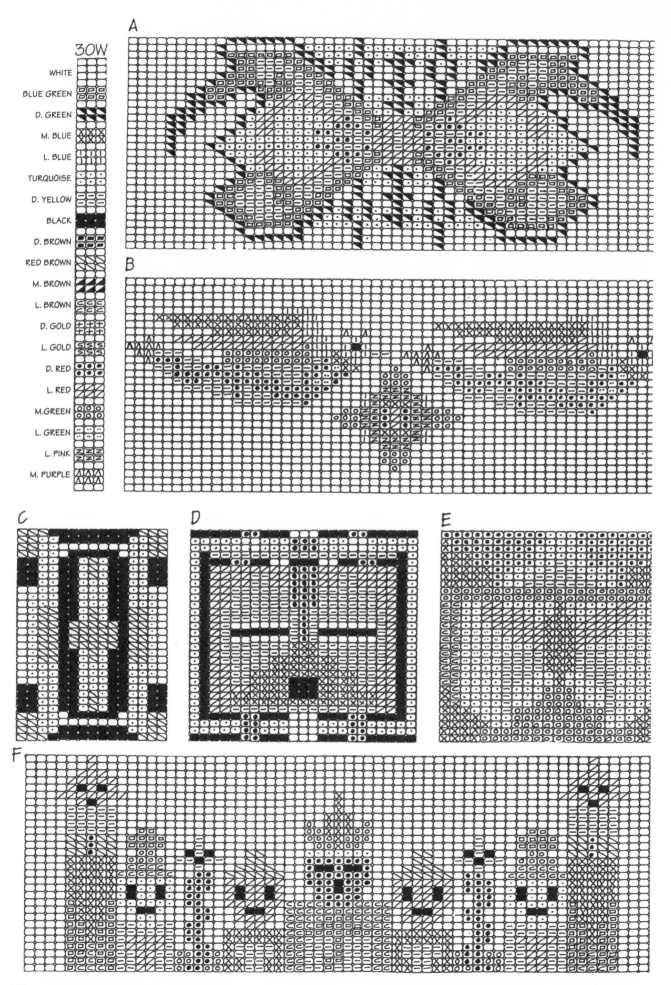

30W

WHITE
BLUE GREEN
D. GREEN
M. BLUE
L. BLUE
TURQUOISE
D. YELLOW
BLACK
D. BROWN
RED BROWN
M. BROWN
L. BROWN
D. GOLD
L. GOLD
D. RED
L. RED
M.GREEN
L. GREEN
L. PINK
M. PURPLE

A

B

C

D

E

F

22

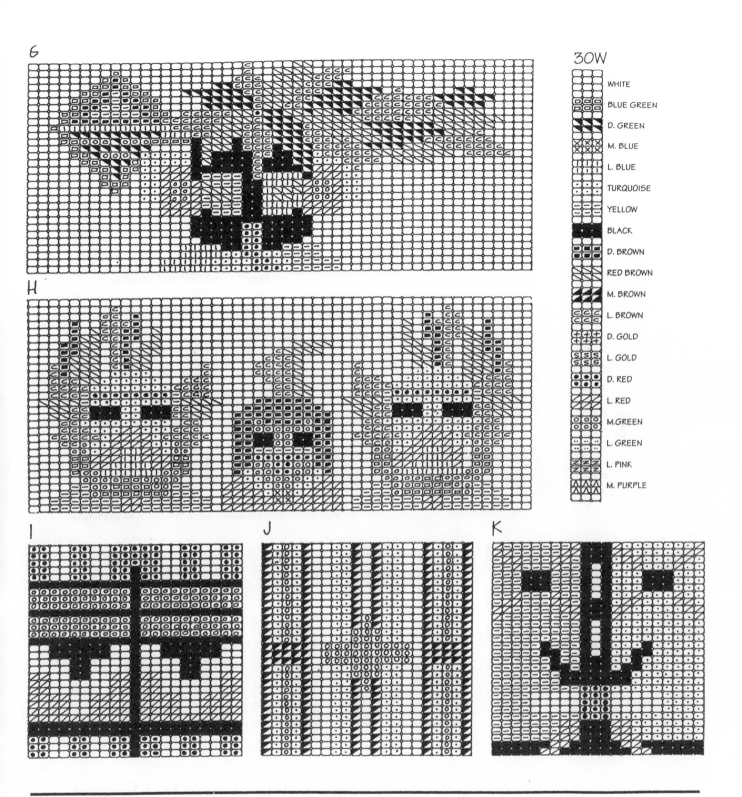

30W SERIES

Designs A–Z on pages 22–25 are all 30 beads wide. Each design can be repeated or they may be used interchangeably until you achieve your desired length. For example, you could begin with a geometric design, then bead a kachina face and return to the same geometric design, alternating designs until you achieve your desired length. If you like, you can separate the designs with several rows of color. The possibilities are numerous.

If you would like to see these designs in color, make copies, color them, cut them apart, and arrange them in the order that you prefer.

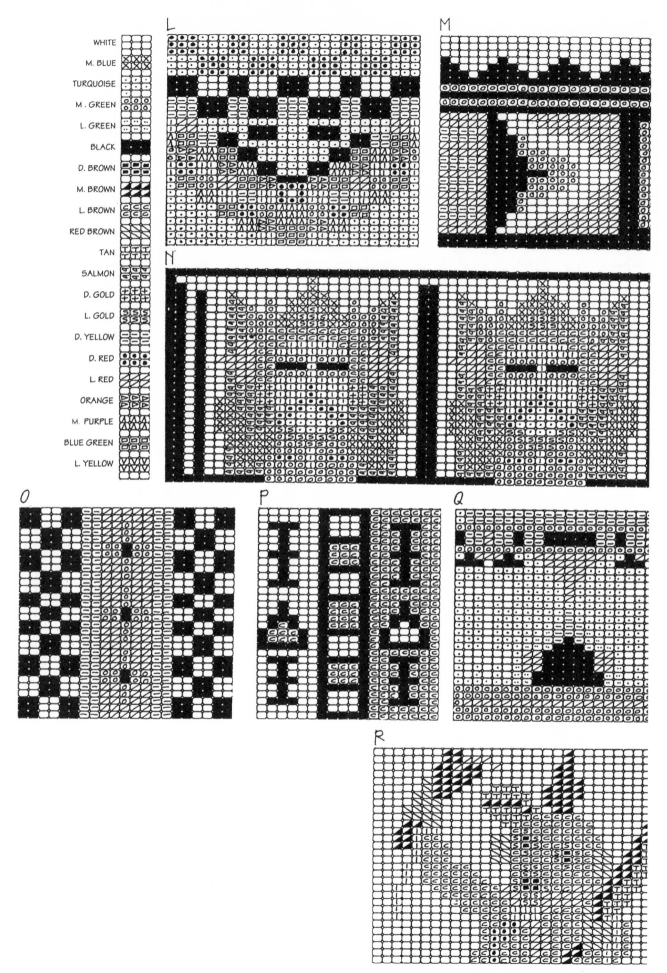

WHITE
M. BLUE
TURQUOISE
M. GREEN
L. GREEN
BLACK
D. BROWN
M. BROWN
L. BROWN
RED BROWN
TAN
SALMON
D. GOLD
L. GOLD
D. YELLOW
D. RED
L. RED
ORANGE
M. PURPLE
BLUE GREEN
L. YELLOW

L

M

N

O

P

Q

R

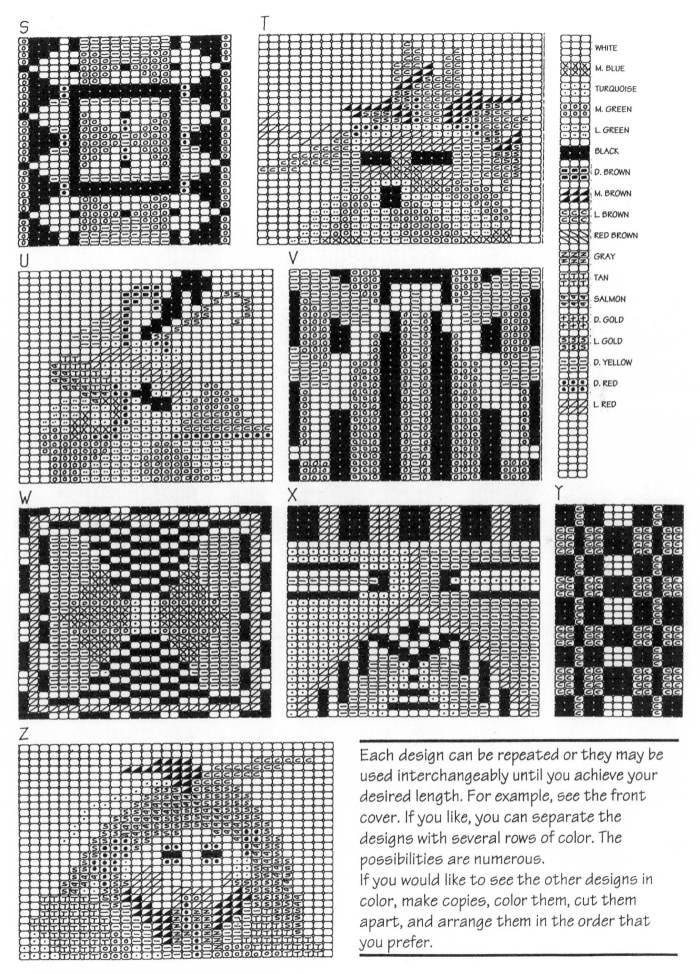

Each design can be repeated or they may be used interchangeably until you achieve your desired length. For example, see the front cover. If you like, you can separate the designs with several rows of color. The possibilities are numerous.

If you would like to see the other designs in color, make copies, color them, cut them apart, and arrange them in the order that you prefer.

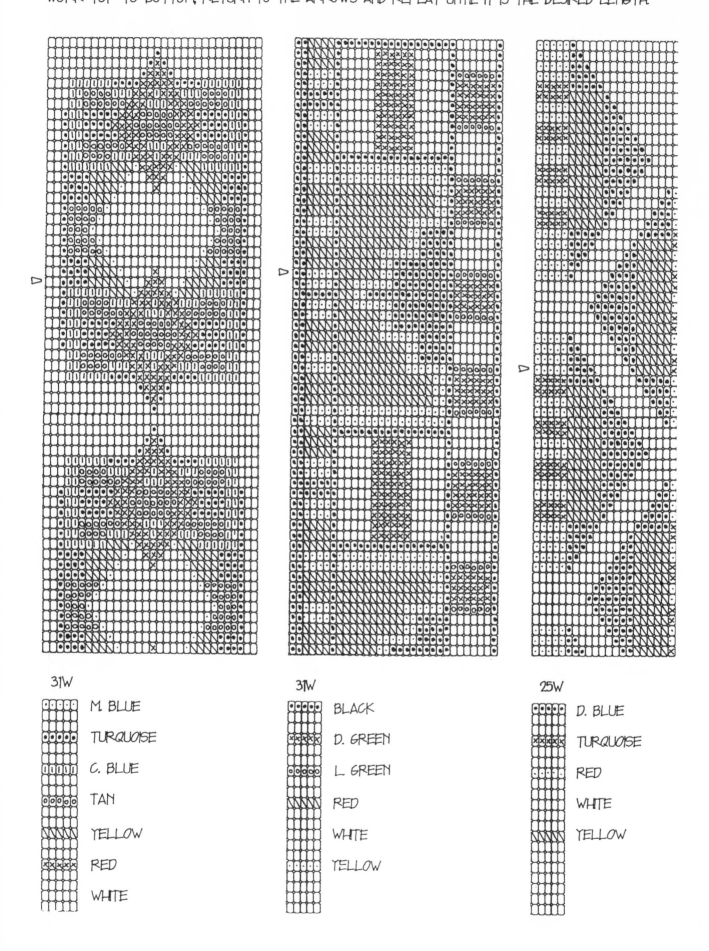

31W

	M. BLUE
	TURQUOISE
	C. BLUE
	TAN
	YELLOW
	RED
	WHITE

31W

	BLACK
	D. GREEN
	L. GREEN
	RED
	WHITE
	YELLOW

25W

	D. BLUE
	TURQUOISE
	RED
	WHITE
	YELLOW

WORK TOP TO BOTTOM. RETURN TO THE ARROWS AND REPEAT UNTIL IT IS THE DESIRED LENGTH.

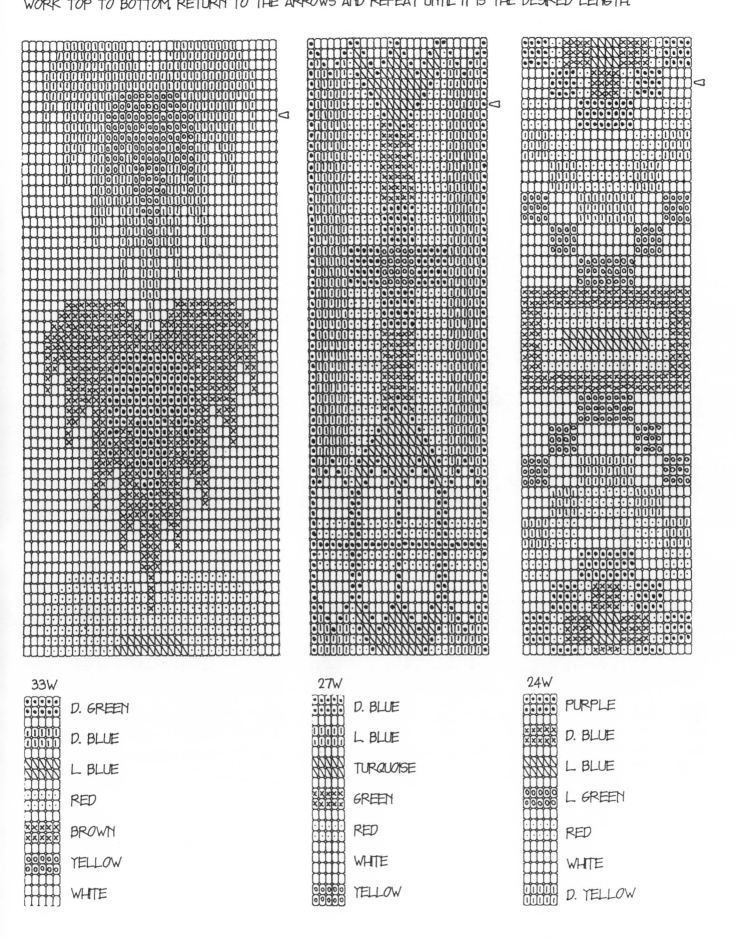

33W
- D. GREEN
- D. BLUE
- L BLUE
- RED
- BROWN
- YELLOW
- WHITE

27W
- D. BLUE
- L BLUE
- TURQUOISE
- GREEN
- RED
- WHITE
- YELLOW

24W
- PURPLE
- D. BLUE
- L BLUE
- L GREEN
- RED
- WHITE
- D. YELLOW

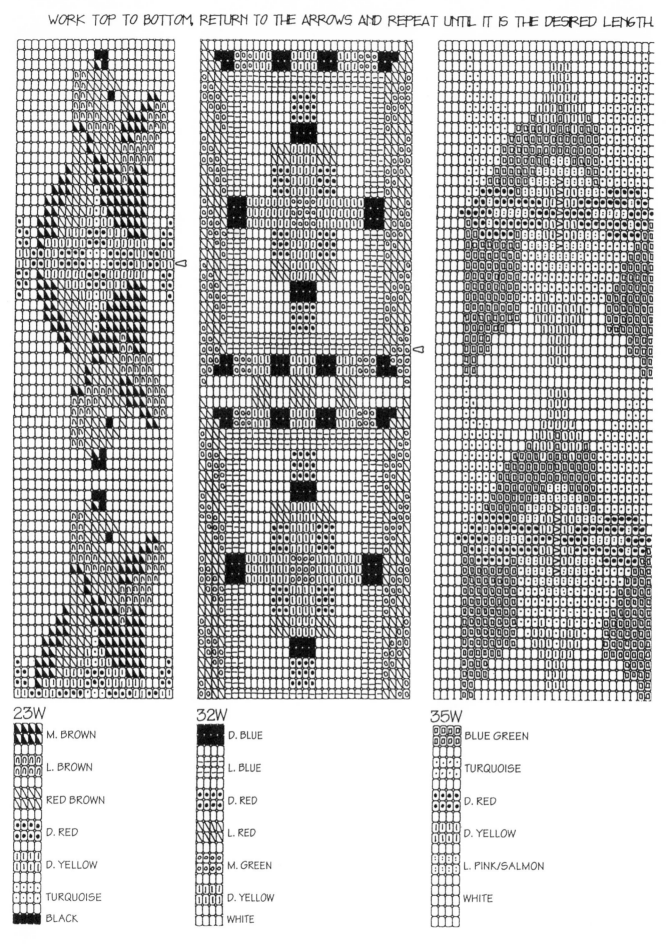

23W

- M. BROWN
- L. BROWN
- RED BROWN
- D. RED
- D. YELLOW
- TURQUOISE
- BLACK

32W

- D. BLUE
- L. BLUE
- D. RED
- L. RED
- M. GREEN
- D. YELLOW
- WHITE

35W

- BLUE GREEN
- TURQUOISE
- D. RED
- D. YELLOW
- L. PINK/SALMON
- WHITE

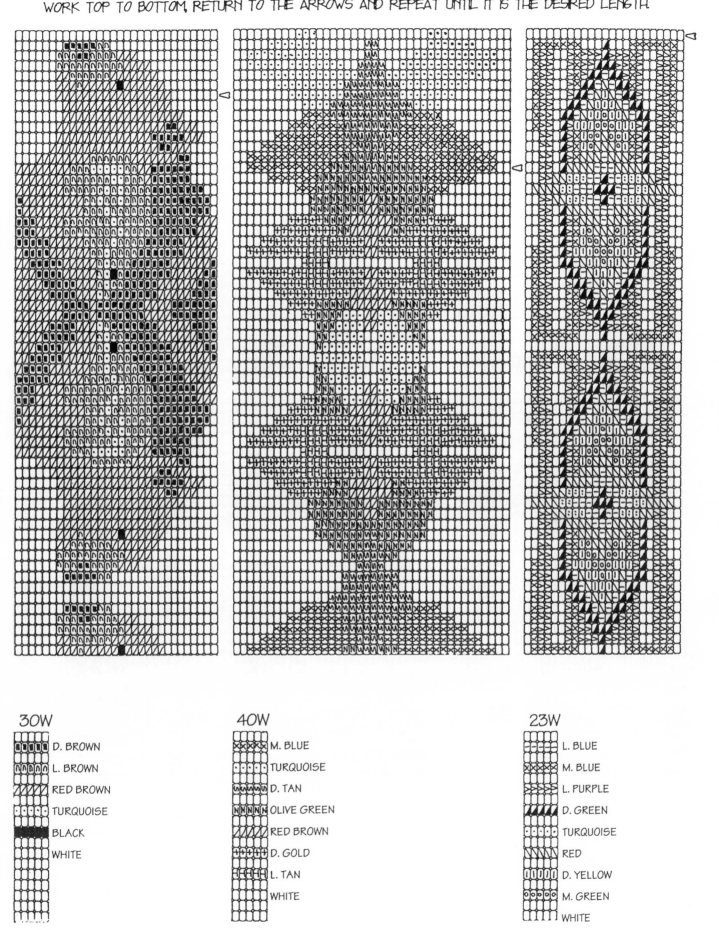

30W

Symbol	Color
	D. BROWN
	L. BROWN
	RED BROWN
	TURQUOISE
	BLACK
	WHITE

40W

Symbol	Color
	M. BLUE
	TURQUOISE
	D. TAN
	OLIVE GREEN
	RED BROWN
	D. GOLD
	L. TAN
	WHITE

23W

Symbol	Color
	L. BLUE
	M. BLUE
	L. PURPLE
	D. GREEN
	TURQUOISE
	RED
	D. YELLOW
	M. GREEN
	WHITE

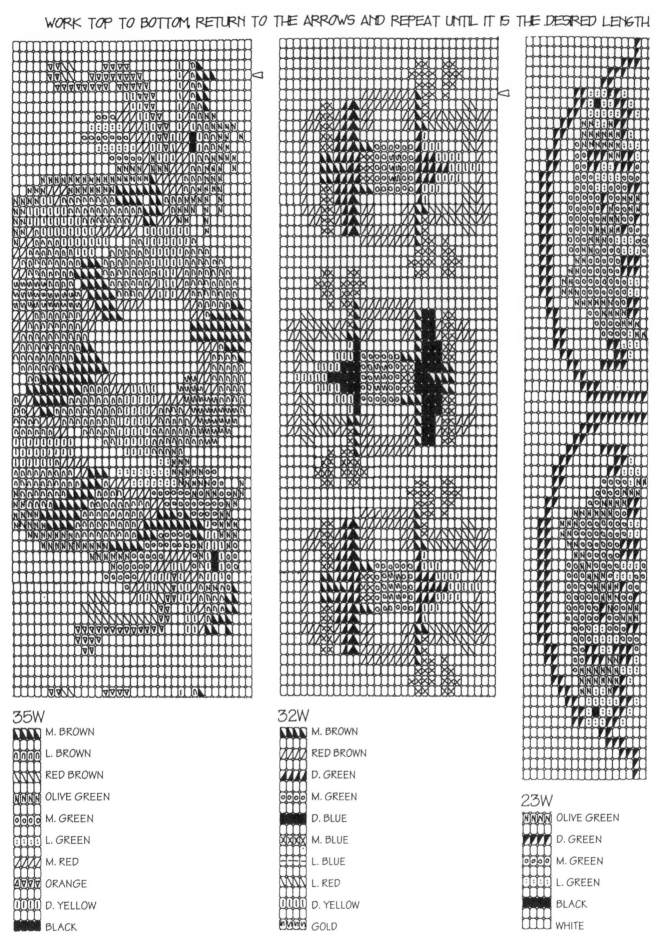

35W

M. BROWN
L. BROWN
RED BROWN
OLIVE GREEN
M. GREEN
L. GREEN
M. RED
ORANGE
D. YELLOW
BLACK

32W

M. BROWN
RED BROWN
D. GREEN
M. GREEN
D. BLUE
M. BLUE
L. BLUE
L. RED
D. YELLOW
GOLD

23W

OLIVE GREEN
D. GREEN
M. GREEN
L. GREEN
BLACK
WHITE

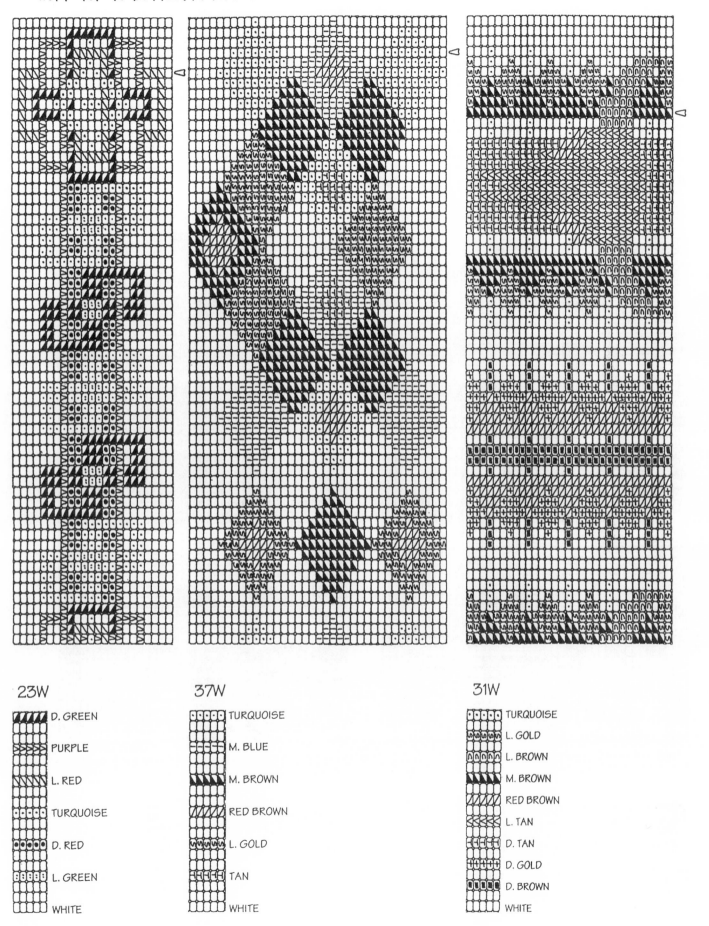

23W

- D. GREEN
- PURPLE
- L. RED
- TURQUOISE
- D. RED
- L. GREEN
- WHITE

37W

- TURQUOISE
- M. BLUE
- M. BROWN
- RED BROWN
- L. GOLD
- TAN
- WHITE

31W

- TURQUOISE
- L. GOLD
- L. BROWN
- M. BROWN
- RED BROWN
- L. TAN
- D. TAN
- D. GOLD
- D. BROWN
- WHITE

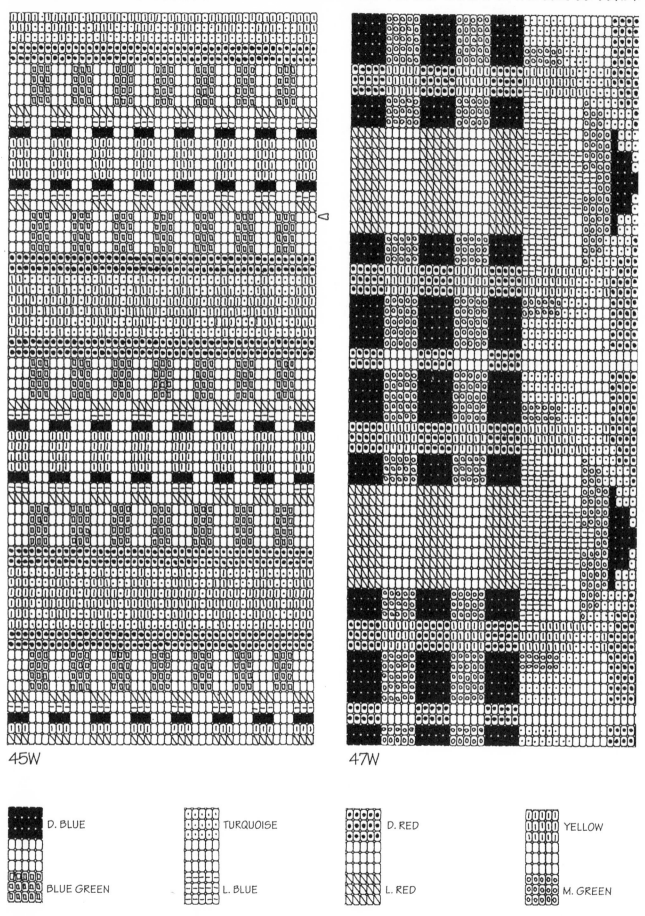

45W

47W

D. BLUE

BLUE GREEN

TURQUOISE

L. BLUE

D. RED

L. RED

YELLOW

M. GREEN

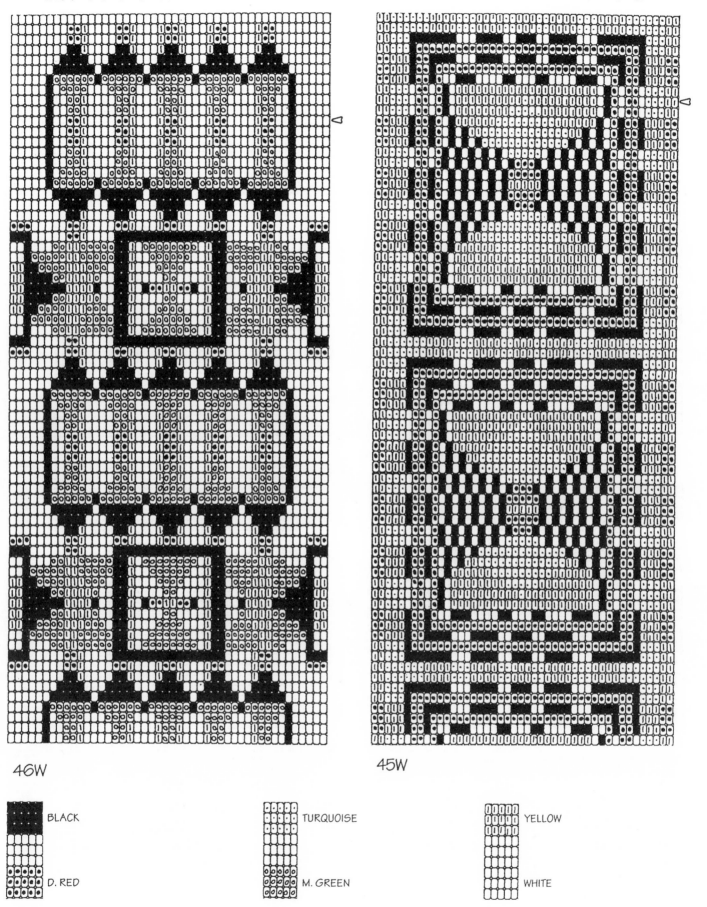

46W

45W

BLACK

TURQUOISE

YELLOW

D. RED

M. GREEN

WHITE

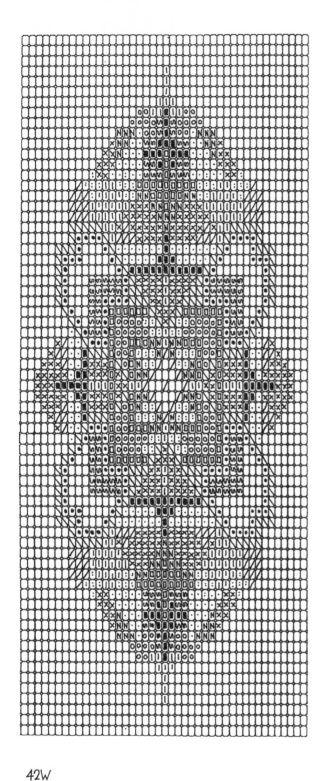

WHITE BACKGROUND

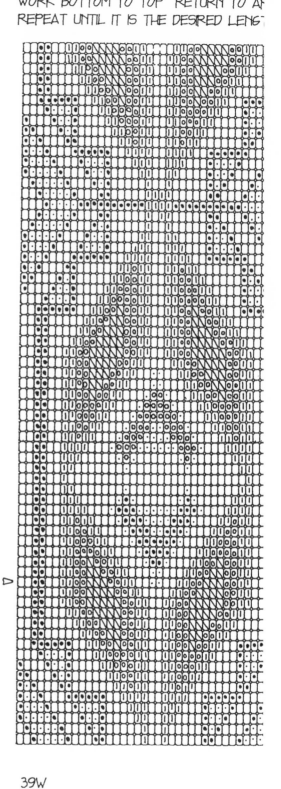

42W

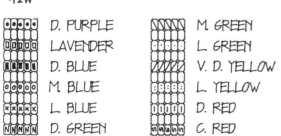

D. PURPLE		M. GREEN	
LAVENDER		L. GREEN	
D. BLUE		V. D. YELLOW	
M. BLUE		L. YELLOW	
L. BLUE		D. RED	
D. GREEN		C. RED	

39W

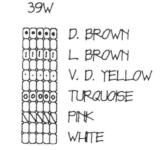

D. BROWN
L. BROWN
V. D. YELLOW
TURQUOISE
PINK
WHITE

WORK TOP TO BOTTOM, RETURN TO THE ARROWS AND REPEAT UNTIL IT IS THE DESIRED LENGTH.

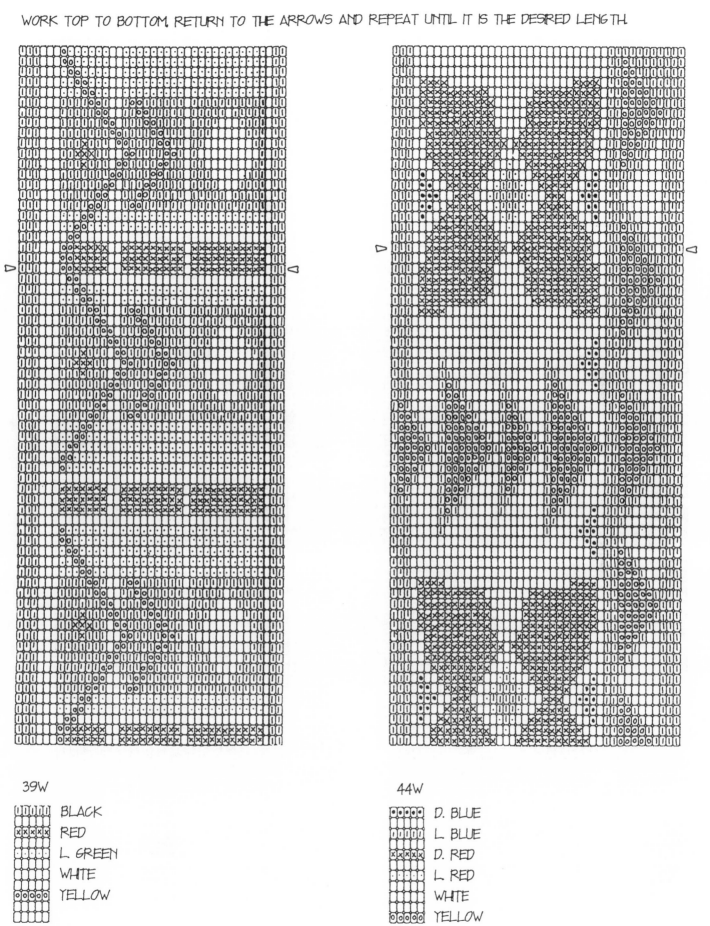

39W

	BLACK
	RED
	L. GREEN
	WHITE
	YELLOW

44W

	D. BLUE
	L. BLUE
	D. RED
	L. RED
	WHITE
	YELLOW

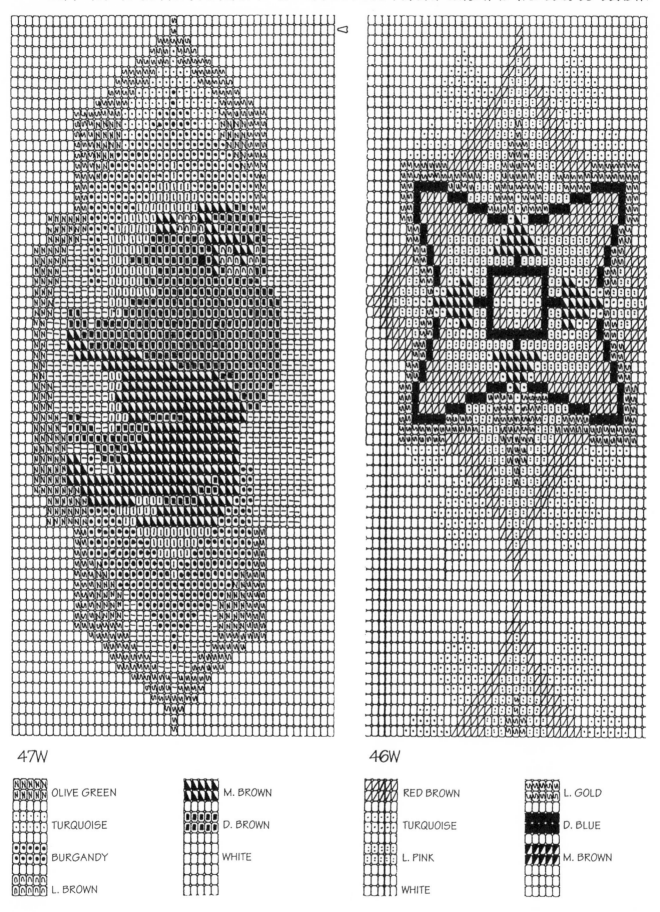

47W

46W

OLIVE GREEN		M. BROWN	
TURQUOISE		D. BROWN	
BURGANDY		WHITE	
L. BROWN			

RED BROWN		L. GOLD	
TURQUOISE		D. BLUE	
L. PINK		M. BROWN	
WHITE			

WORK TOP TO BOTTOM, RETURN TO THE ARROWS AND REPEAT UNTIL IT IS THE DESIRED LENGTH.

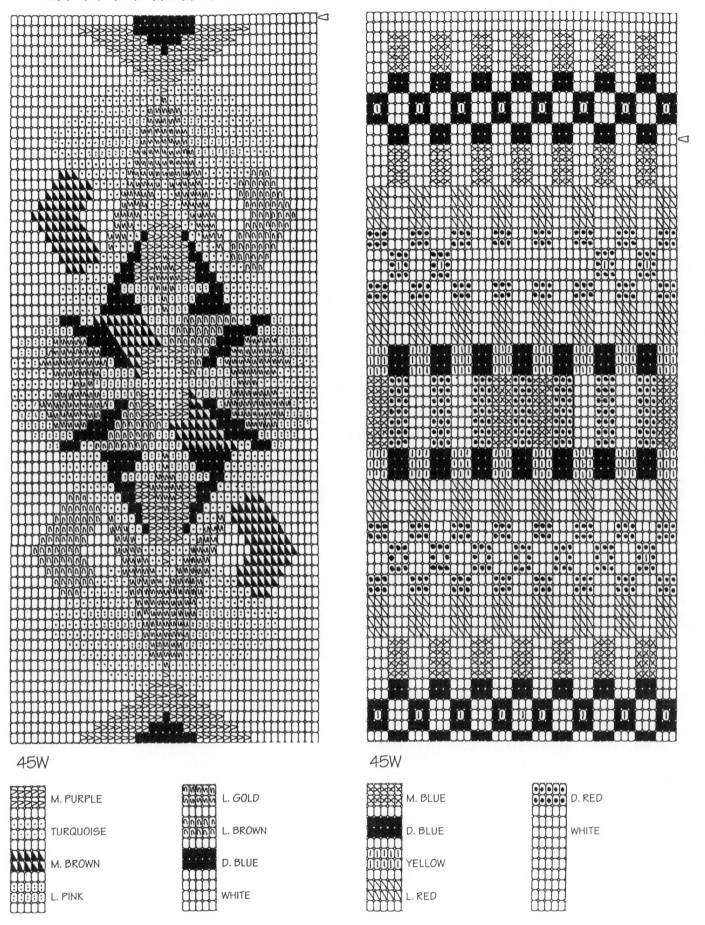

45W

45W

M. PURPLE

TURQUOISE

M. BROWN

L. PINK

L. GOLD

L. BROWN

D. BLUE

WHITE

M. BLUE

D. BLUE

YELLOW

L. RED

D. RED

WHITE

37

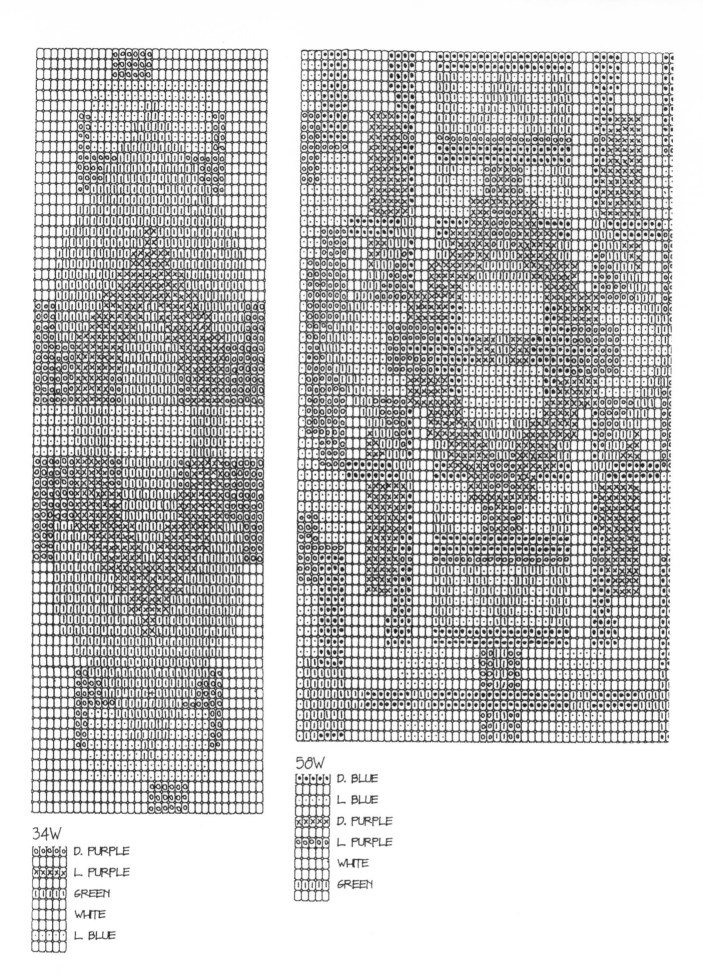

34W

	D. PURPLE
	L PURPLE
	GREEN
	WHITE
	L BLUE

58W

	D. BLUE
	L BLUE
	D. PURPLE
	L PURPLE
	WHITE
	GREEN

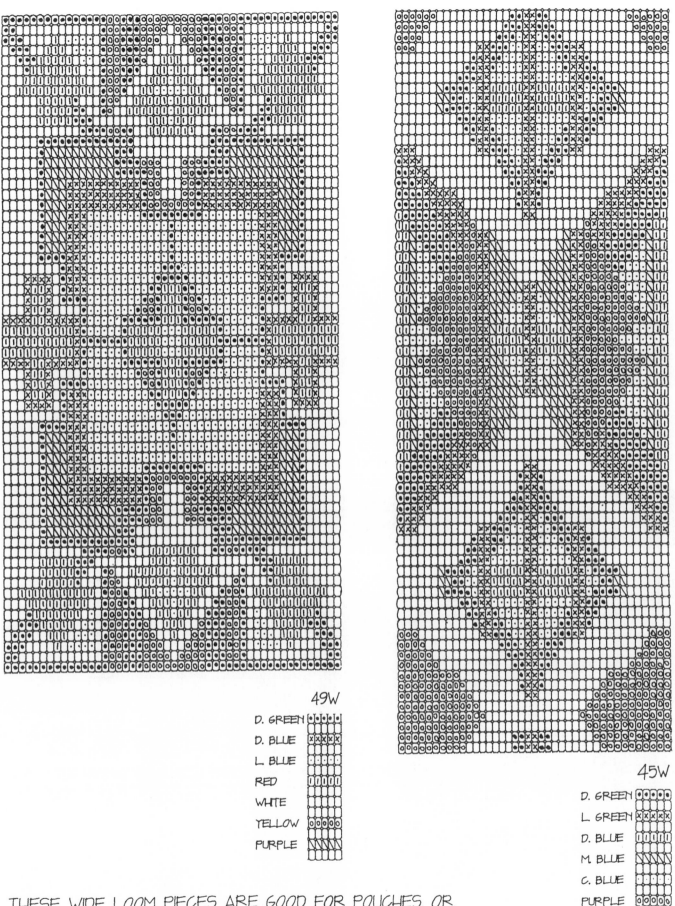

49W

D. GREEN	·|·|·|·|·
D. BLUE	x|x|x|x|x
L. BLUE	·|·|·|·|·
RED	⏇|⏇|⏇|⏇|⏇
WHITE					
YELLOW	o|o|o|o|o
PURPLE	⧄|⧄|⧄|⧄|⧄

45W

D. GREEN	●|●|●|●|●
L. GREEN	x|x|x|x|x
D. BLUE	⏇|⏇|⏇|⏇|⏇
M. BLUE	⧄|⧄|⧄|⧄|⧄
C. BLUE	·|·|·|·|·
PURPLE	o|o|o|o|o

THESE WIDE LOOM PIECES ARE GOOD FOR POUCHES. OR,
KEEP REPEATING UNTIL IT IS THE DESIRED LENGTH.

52W

■ ■ ■		BLACK
⟋⟋⟋		RED BROW
⊂⊂⊂		L. BROWN
▦▦▦		D. BROWN
ⲦⲦⲦ		TAN
◪◪◪		D. GREEN
⊙⊙⊙		M. GREEN
∙∙∙		TURQUOIS
✕✕✕		M. BLUE
∥∥∥		L. BLUE
⦿⦿⦿		D. RED
⟋⟋⟋		L. RED
⊏⊐⊏		D. YELLOW
		WHITE

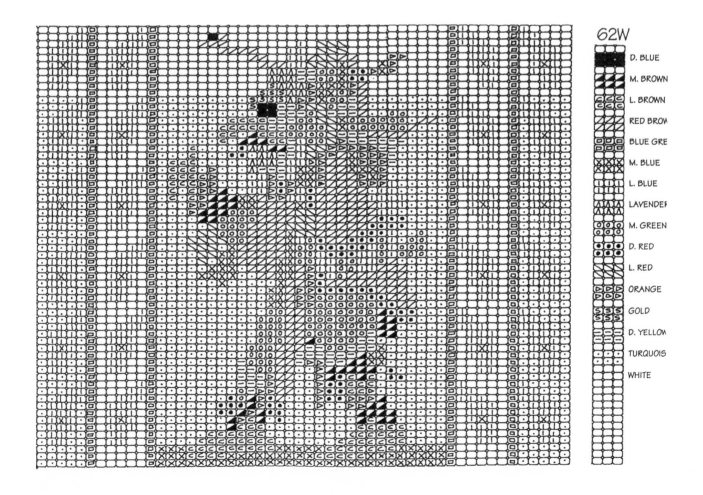

62W

■ ■ ■		D. BLUE
◪◪◪		M. BROWN
⊂⊂⊂		L. BROWN
⟋⟋⟋		RED BROW
▣▣▣		BLUE GRE
✕✕✕		M. BLUE
∥∥∥		L. BLUE
ΛΛΛ		LAVENDER
⊙⊙⊙		M. GREEN
⦿⦿⦿		D. RED
⟋⟋⟋		L. RED
▷▷▷		ORANGE
⑀⑀⑀		GOLD
⊏⊐⊏		D. YELLOW
∙∙∙		TURQUOIS
		WHITE

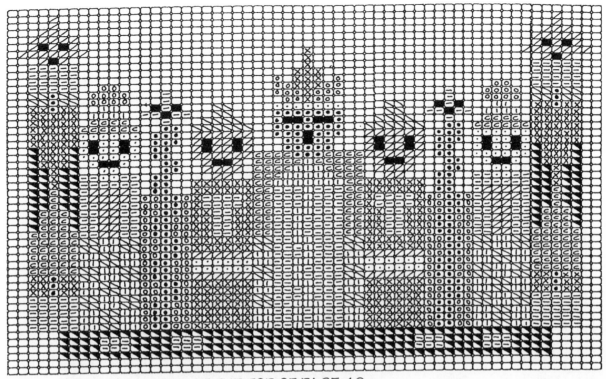

52W   SEE COLOR CODE AT THE TOP OF PAGE 40.

71W

RED BROWN	
M. BROWN	
L. BROWN	
D. GOLD	
L. GOLD	
D. TAN	
L. TAN	
OLIVE GREEN	
L. GREEN	
D. YELLOW	
L. YELLOW	
D. RED	
L. RED	
M. BLUE	
TURQUOISE	
WHITE	

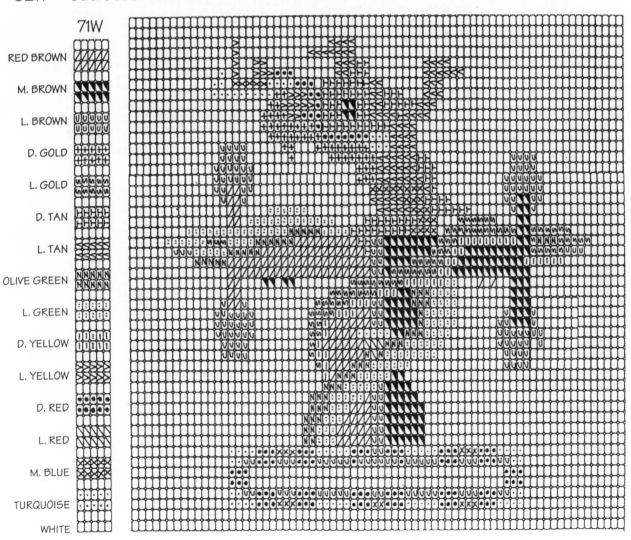

Work left to right.

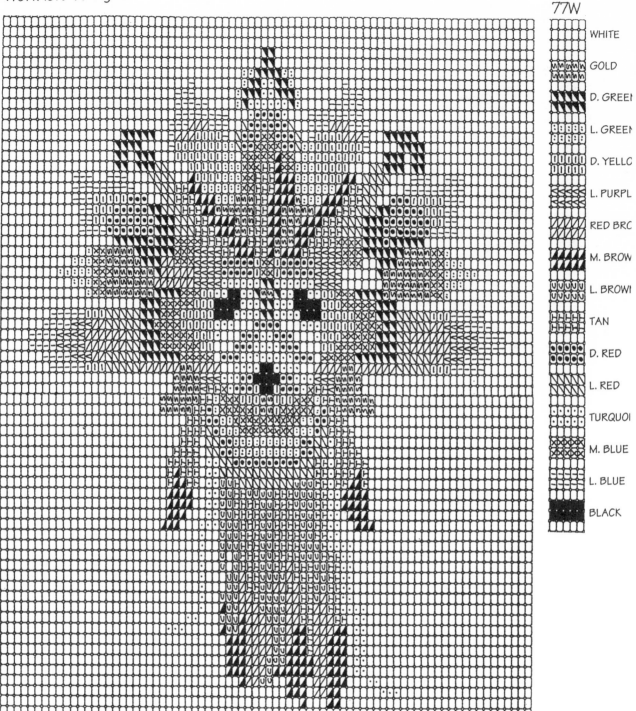

77W

	WHITE
	GOLD
	D. GREEN
	L. GREEN
	D. YELLO
	L. PURPL
	RED BRC
	M. BROW
	L. BROWI
	TAN
	D. RED
	L. RED
	TURQUOI
	M. BLUE
	L. BLUE
	BLACK

98W   This is the color code for the design on page 43.

	D. BROWN		TAN		D. RED		M. BLUE
	M. BROWN		L. TAN		L. RED		L. BLUE
	BLACK		YELLOW		D. GREEN		TURQUOISE

42

43

60W

BLACK

D. GREEN

D. BROWN

ORANGE

V. D. RED

L. RED

TURQUOISE

BEIGE

WHITE

GRAY

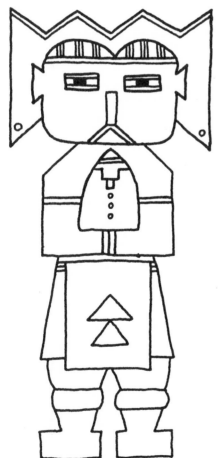

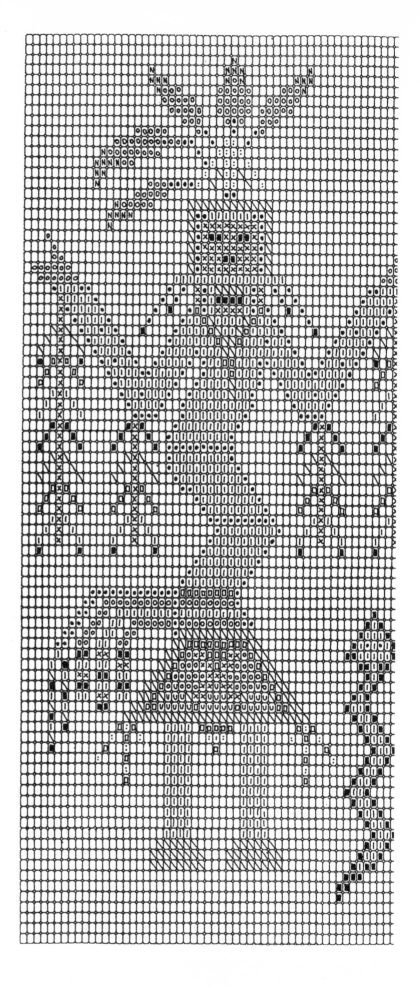

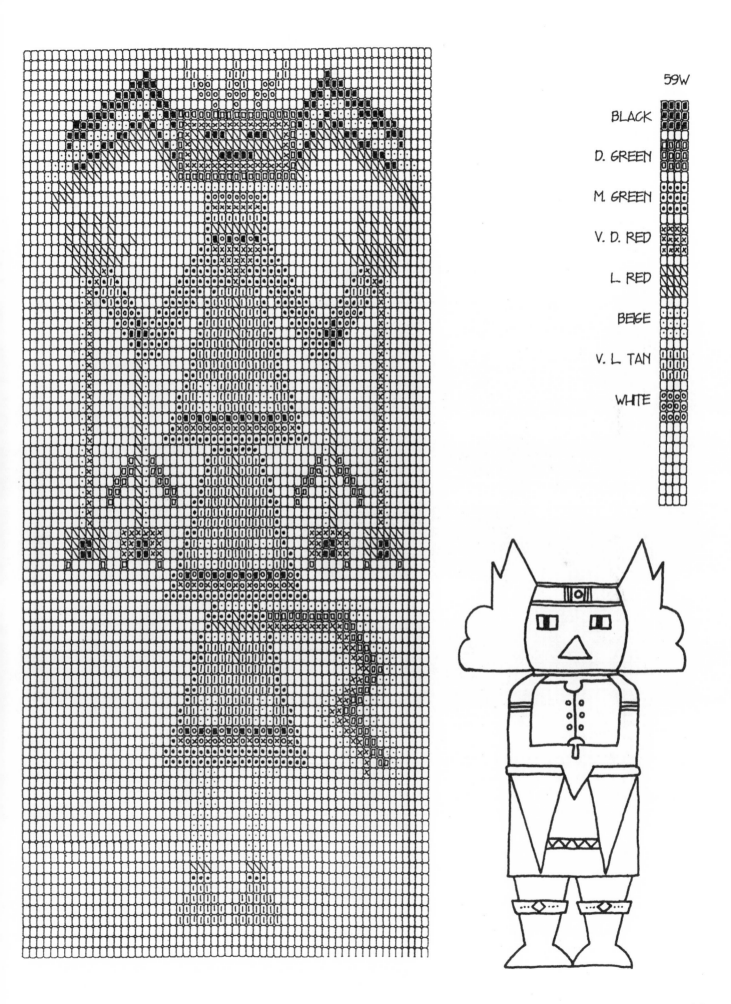

59W

BLACK

D. GREEN

M. GREEN

V. D. RED

L. RED

BEIGE

V. L. TAN

WHITE

45

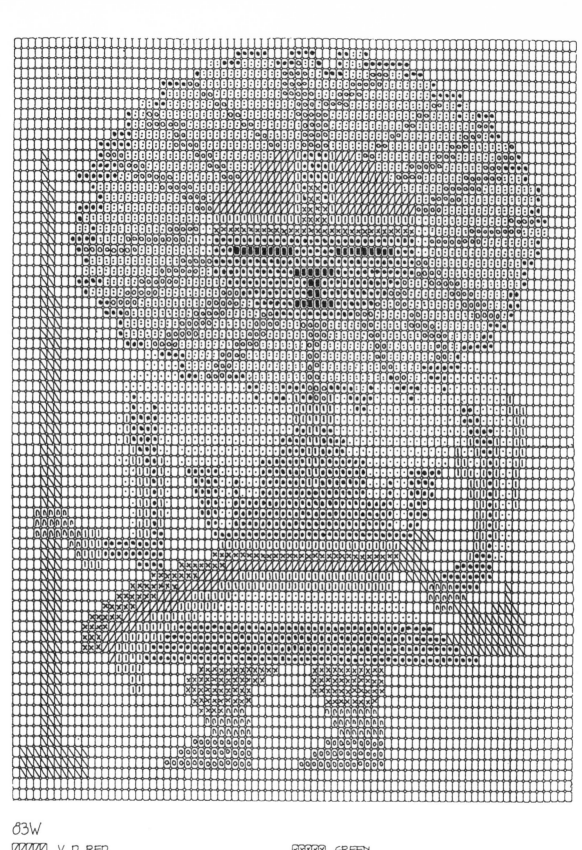

83W

///// V. D. RED	XXXXX GREEN
•••••• RED	WHITE
○○○○○ D. ORANGE	\\\\ M. BROWN
⊓⊓⊓⊓⊓ L. ORANGE	∩∩∩∩∩ L. BROWN
IIIII D. BLUE	▮▮▮▮▮ BLACK
L. BLUE	

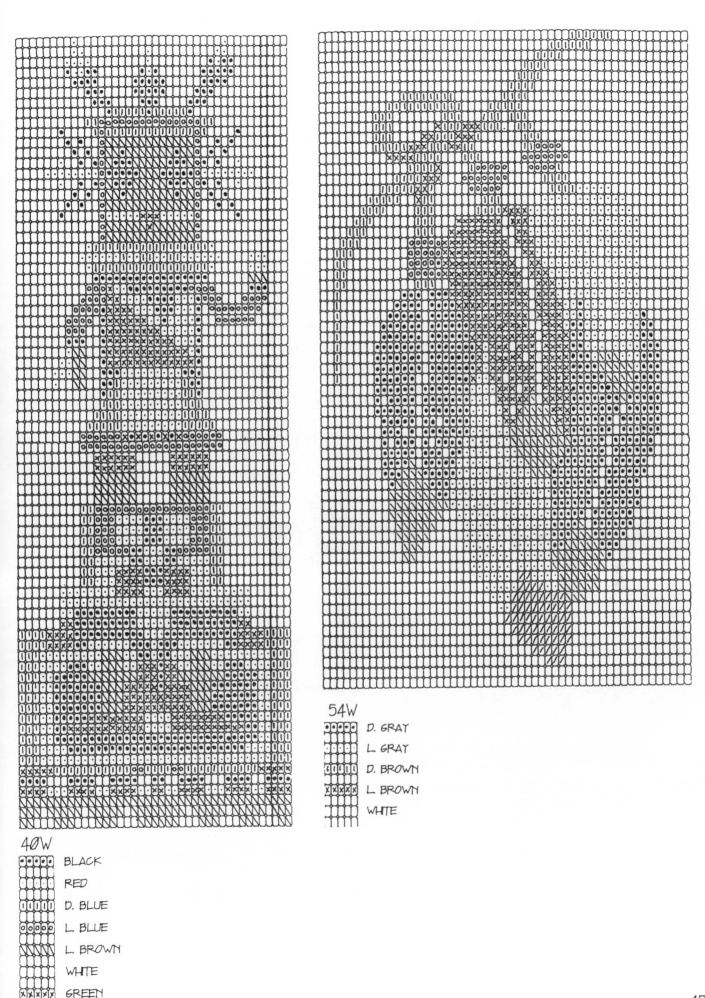

54W

●●●●	D. GRAY
·····	L GRAY
◍◍◍◍◍	D. BROWN
xxxxx	L BROWN
⊥⊥⊥⊥⊥	WHITE

40W

●●●●●	BLACK
·····	RED
◍◍◍◍◍	D. BLUE
○○○○○	L BLUE
⁄⁄⁄⁄⁄	L. BROWN
⊥⊥⊥⊥⊥	WHITE
xxxxx	GREEN

A.

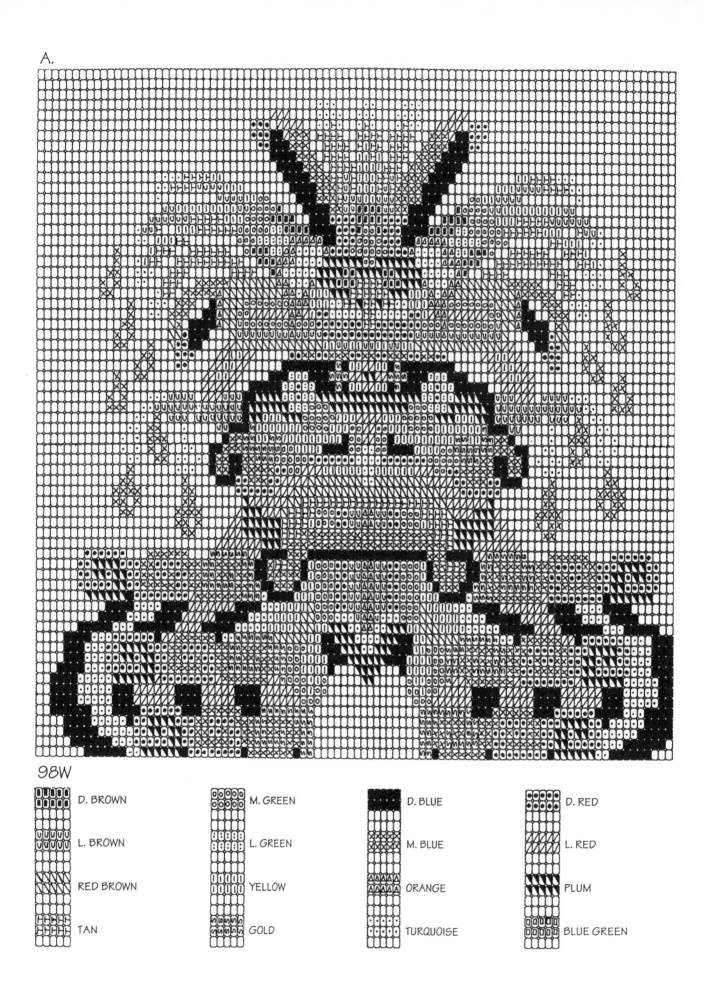

98W

D. BROWN	M. GREEN	D. BLUE	D. RED
L. BROWN	L. GREEN	M. BLUE	L. RED
RED BROWN	YELLOW	ORANGE	PLUM
TAN	GOLD	TURQUOISE	BLUE GREEN

B.

98W   Use Color Code on page 48

Both of these designs would make great pouches. Since both graphs are 98W, you can use both designs for one pouch—one design on each side. Or, you can use them separately. If you want to have the beadwork all in one piece, start beading Design B at the top and work to the bottom. Then bead enough rows to make up the bottom of your bag. Once you finish that, begin beading Design A from the bottom to the top, beading from right to left. (Or, turn the design upside down and work left to right.) You can dictate the length of your bag by adding or subtracting rows of beads in your background color at the top of the design.

You have the option of working Design A as shown or, for a narrower piece, begin at the arrow-marked row and bead t
next arrow. You can use Design A (color code on page 51) by itself or combine it with Design C. If you combine them t
make one long strip of beadwork, start at the top of Design A and bead left to right. Work until you reach the row m.
with the O—begin at this row with Design B. Continue from B through C.

If you want to make a pouch that is all one piece of beadwork and covers both sides with Designs A–C, follow directic
above. When you finish, continue the pattern at the bottom of Design C until it is wide enough to cover the bottom c
bag. Then turn the graph upside down and work left to right, starting at the bottom of C and working up through A.

B

C

95W

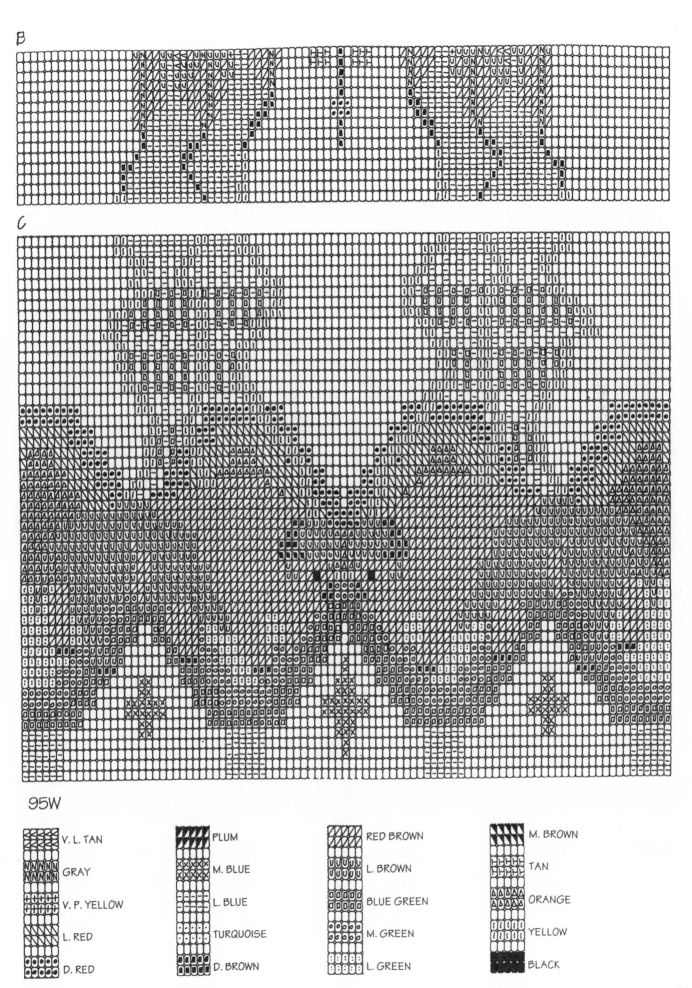

	V. L. TAN		PLUM		RED BROWN		M. BROWN
	GRAY		M. BLUE		L. BROWN		TAN
	V. P. YELLOW		L. BLUE		BLUE GREEN		ORANGE
	L. RED		TURQUOISE		M. GREEN		YELLOW
	D. RED		D. BROWN		L. GREEN		BLACK

THESE WIDE LOOM PIECES ARE GOOD FOR POUCHES.

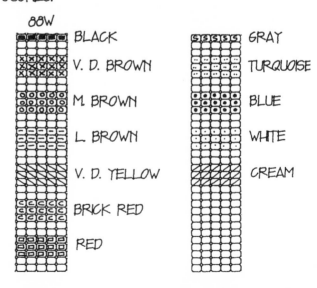

88W

BLACK
V. D. BROWN
M. BROWN
L. BROWN
V. D. YELLOW
BRICK RED
RED

GRAY
TURQUOISE
BLUE
WHITE
CREAM

TO MAKE THIS PIECE LONGER, ADD ROWS TO TOP & BOTTOM IN YOUR BACKGROUND COLOR.

67W

D. BLUE	TURQUOISE	D. GREEN
M. BLUE	C. BLUE	L GREEN

RED
ORANGE

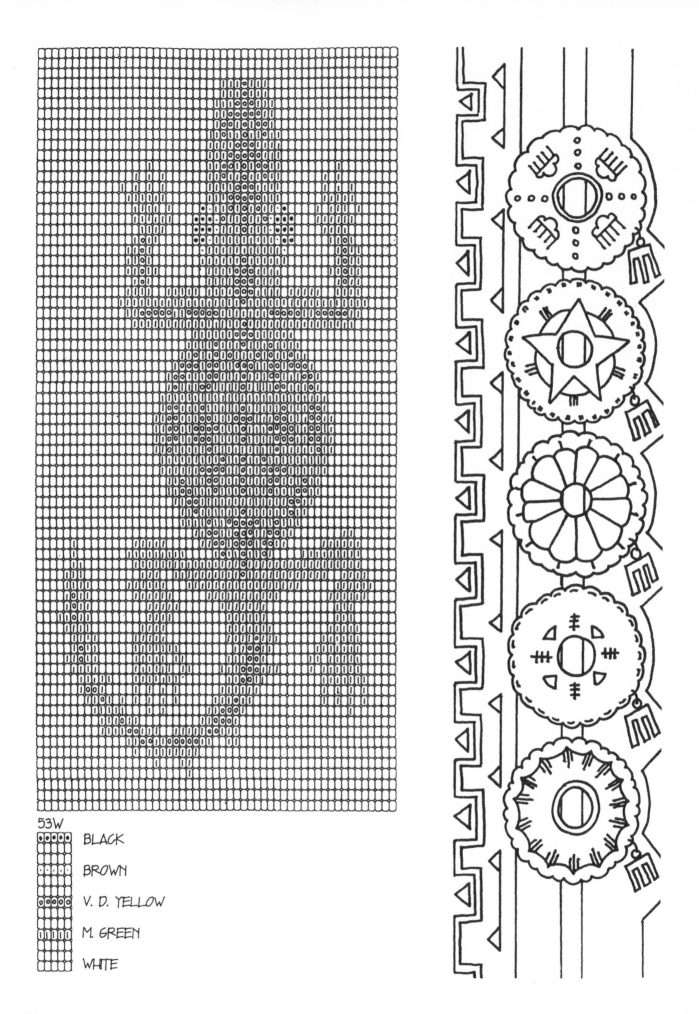

53W

BLACK

BROWN

V. D. YELLOW

M. GREEN

WHITE

69W

X X X X X	V. D. BROWN
I I I I I	M. BROWN
	L. BROWN
• • • • •	BLACK
⟋⟋⟋⟋	GRAY
⊃ ⊃ ⊃ ⊃	WHITE
	D. BLUE
∩ ∩ ∩ ∩	D. YELLOW

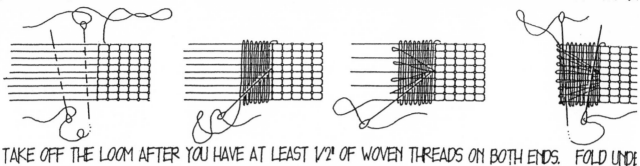

TAKE OFF THE LOOM AFTER YOU HAVE AT LEAST 1/2" OF WOVEN THREADS ON BOTH ENDS.   FOLD UNDE

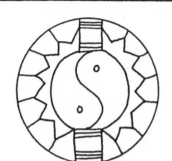

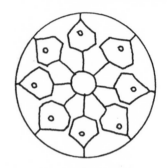

ONCE YOU HAVE FINISHED WEAVING THE ENDS OF YOUR LOOM PIECE AND HAVE FOLDED
THEM UNDER, YOU ARE READY TO SEW YOUR WORK ONTO SOFT LEATHER OR MATERIAL
TO MAKE YOUR BELT OR HATBAND. START IN THE MIDDLE AND SEW SEVERAL INCHES
TO THE RIGHT; THEN, SEVERAL INCHES TO THE LEFT. KEEP ALTERNATING THE DIRECTION
YOU SEW UNTIL YOU REACH BOTH ENDS. SEW LOOSELY. CONSTANTLY CHECK THAT IT IS EVEN.

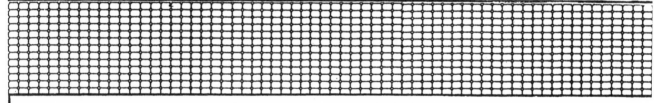

TO TRY THE FOLLOWING YOU MUST ALLOW ENOUGH ROOM ON YOUR LEATHER OR MATERIAL

For example: The full waist measurement for your belt is 25 inches. You will need to allow enough material for attaching a belt
buckle or for overlapping and lacing with a concho or an old button. Allow at least one inch on both ends. Measure how many
rows you want to extend the design and allow for that space between the buckle and the loom work. If you want to extend the
design an inch allow another inch on both ends. Your loomwork will be (25 inches minus 4 inches) 21 inches long.

EXTEND PART OF THE DESIGN ONTO YOUR LEATHER BY SEWING ROWS OF BEADS. 2 BEADS AT A TIME, FROM T
END OF THE LOOMWORK OUTWARDS

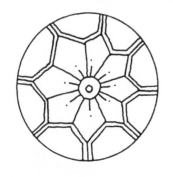

TO TRANSFER THE APPLIQUE DESIGNS TO LEATHER OR MATERIAL, TRACE THE DESIGNS ONTO TRACING PAPER (WAX PAPER WORKS). LAY THE TRACING OVER YOUR MATERIAL. PUNCH HOLES ALONG THE LINES WITH A FINE TIP FELT PEN, LEAVING A SMALL INK DOT. (I USE AN ALMOST DRY FELT TIP. YOU WILL END UP COVERING ANY LINES WITH BEADS OR THREAD.) REMOVE THE PAPER. CONNECT THE DOTS.

TO ENLARGE OR REDUCE A DESIGN, USE A PHOTOCOPIER.

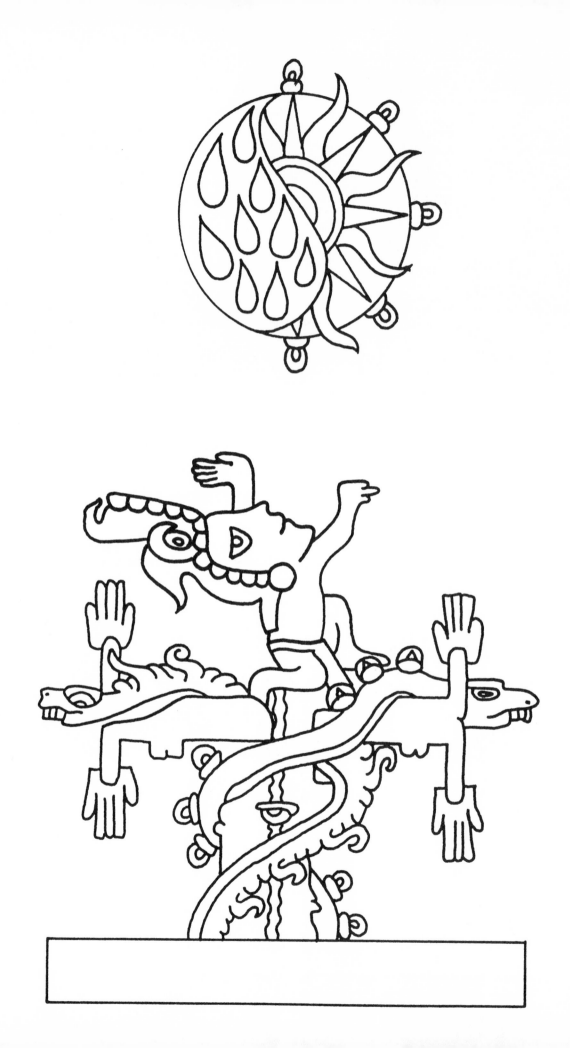

THESE TWO DESIGNS WERE ORGIN[A]
DONE FOR A STAINED GLASS PROJE[CT]
THEY ARE DRAWN STRUCTURALLY [LIKE]
STAINED GLASS WINDOWS.

VISUALIZE WORLD

PEACEPEACEPEACEPEACEPEACE   PEACEPEACEPEACE.PEACEPEA[CE]

66

REMINDER

REDUCE OR ENLARGE THESE DESIGNS AS NEEDED. MAKE COPIES AND USE THEM LIKE
YOU WOULD A COLORING BOOK. THIS WILL HELP WHEN IT'S TIME TO CHOSE COLORS.

THE TREE PLANTER AND THE LOGGER

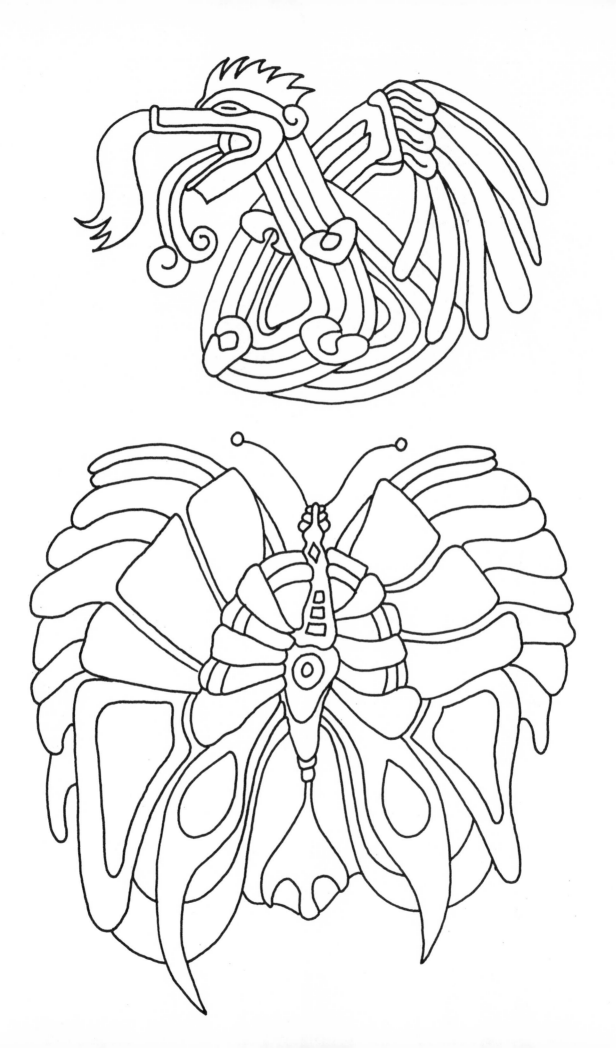